CHAMPION OF FREEDOM

Nelson Mandela

Nelson Mandela

Kem Knapp Sawyer

Greensboro, North Carolina

Scottish Geographical Magazine, 1885.

To Jon,
to Kate, Brian, Eve, Dan, and Ida,
and to my grandchildren, Karenna, Jack, Thomas, Julia, and Raya

Champion of Freedom
Nelson Mandela
Copyright © 2012 by Morgan Reynolds Publishing

Library of Congress Cataloging-in-Publication Data

Sawyer, Kem Knapp.
 Champion of freedom : Nelson Mandela / by Kem Knapp Sawyer.
   p. cm.
 ISBN 978-1-59935-167-4 ISBN 978-1-59935-312-8 (ebook)
 1. Mandela, Nelson, 1918- 2. Presidents--South Africa--Biography. 3.
Political prisoners--South Africa--Biography. 4. Apartheid--South Africa.
5. South Africa--Politics and government--20th century. I. Title.
 DT1974.S29 2011
 968.06'5092--dc22
 [B]

                           2010054478

Printed in the United States of America
First Edition

Book cover and interior designed by:
Ed Morgan, navyblue design studio
Greensboro, NC

Table of Contents

one

Son of a Village Chief

At the age of sixteen, Nelson Mandela prepared to take part in a time-honored ritual to mark his passage to manhood. He and other boys from his tiny village in South Africa had already spent days at their initiation school, learning about their heritage as Xhosa people. Now it was time to take the next step: circumcision. Without circumcision, a youth could not marry, start a family, inherit his father's wealth, or participate in tribal councils.

"At dawn, when the stars were still in the sky, we began our preparation," Mandela later recalled. "We were escorted to the river to bathe in its cold waters, a ritual that signified our purification before the ceremony."

At the moment of circumcision, Mandela was expected to shout "*Ndiyindoda!*"—"I am a man!" There would be no anesthesia. The initiates were supposed to bear the pain in silence—a testament to their bravery, intense discipline, and willingness to subject themselves to the requirements of their society. Mandela shouted *Ndiyindoda*! But he had hesitated and then worried that someone might think he was not brave. "I felt ashamed," Mandela wrote years later, "because the other boys seemed much stronger and braver than I had been."

In time, though, no one in his small village—or the world over—would doubt the bravery of Nelson Mandela.

When Nelson Mandela was born, on July 18, 1918, he was named Rolihlahla (pronounced *Roli-shla-shla*). His parents lived in Mvezo, a tiny village on the Mbashe River in an area known as the Transkei (now the Eastern Cape). The villagers were from the Thembu tribe of the Xhosa nation. The Xhosa had lived in the area for hundreds of years and comprised a number of clans, including the Thembu.

Mandela's father, Gadla Henry Mphakanyiswa— "a tall, dark-skinned man with a straight and stately posture"—served as village chief. Chief Henry knew the history of his people, his memory was prodigious, and he was a renowned storyteller. The entire community looked to him for guidance. He had earned their respect.

The villagers considered Chief Henry a relatively wealthy man, as evidenced by his four wives, each of whom lived with her children in her own homestead, or *kraal*, an enclosed area with a thatched hut and a field where crops grew and animals grazed. Mandela was one of thirteen children, the oldest child of his father's third wife, Nosekeni Fanny.

Chief Henry believed that the land that had belonged to his ancestors should be ruled by the Thembu people. But for centuries British colonists and Afrikaners (descendants of the Dutch and French Huguenot settlers who had come to southern Africa beginning in 1652 and whose mother tongue is Afrikaans) had competed for their land. Fighting intensified after gold and diamonds were discovered. The Xhosa fought both the British and the Afrikaners. In 1910, the whites asserted their control with the formation of the Union of South Africa, which became part of the British Commonwealth. The white minority in South Africa elected members to the South African parliament while the British monarchy ruled from afar. Village leaders like Chief Henry had little say.

The first cabinet of the Union of South Africa in 1910 under the leadership of Prime Minister Louis Botha

As chief, Henry thought he owed his allegiance to the Thembu king, not the British government. So when a British-appointed magistrate ordered the chief to appear before him regarding a Mvezo villager who had complained about a stray ox, Chief Henry refused. "My father possessed a proud rebelliousness," Mandela later recalled, "a stubborn sense of fairness." The magistrate punished Chief Henry for insubordination, stripping him of his position and income.

After Mandela's father was deposed as village chief, Nosekeni Fanny and her small children left Mvezo and moved to Qunu to be near relatives who could provide for them. The family settled into their new surroundings, living in three huts made of grass and dirt. One was for cooking, another for sleeping, and the third for storage.

Mandela spent the first few years playing with other boys his own age, many of them his cousins who lived nearby. They climbed on rocks, swam, fished, used sling shots to hunt, and played stick fighting. Mandela loved the freedom to roam; the wide open spaces were invigorating. By the age of five, he was herding cattle and sheep. Cattle were highly prized by the Xhosa, and Mandela too grew fond of them.

Nosekeni taught her son to value generosity and honor his ancestors. She also introduced him to Christian values. Her friends—two Methodist brothers who lived in Qunu—encouraged Nosekeni to baptize the young Mandela and to send him to school. No one in Mandela's family had ever attended school, but Chief Henry decided it was the right thing to do, especially after hearing that the Methodist brothers had described his youngest son as "a clever young fellow."

When Mandela started school at the age of seven he had never worn trousers. His father shortened a pair of his own by cutting the legs off at the knee. They were much too big in the waist so Mandela used a piece of string to hold them up. He set off on the first day of school in his "new" clothes feeling very proud.

The teacher at this one-room school, Miss Mdingane, gave Rolihlahla the English name Nelson. (It was a common practice in those days for schoolteachers to give African children in the mission schools English names.) Nelson studied the same subjects taught in England, was introduced to British culture, and used British textbooks.

Two years later Nelson's father began experiencing coughing fits; he was suffering from an undiagnosed lung disease that would end his life. Nelson was only nine years old. Before dying Chief Henry was assured that his good friend Jongintaba Dalindyebo, "a very noble man," would care for Nelson. (At Chief Henry's urging Jongintaba had been named regent after the death of the Thembu king. Jongintaba felt he owed Chief Henry a favor and had offered to adopt Nelson.)

After his father's death, Nelson moved to Mqhekezweni to the Great Place, where Jongintaba lived with his family. Upon arriving at the royal residence Nelson found himself surrounded by

Mandela never forgot the first time he saw Jongintaba "David" Dalindyebo. The regent drove up in his Ford V8, and a group of tribal elders saluted him, saying "*Bayete* (Hail), Jongintaba!" Young Mandela was awestruck. The family of Jongintaba called Mandela *tatomkhulu*, which translated means grandpa, because they found Mandela to be very serious and they said he looked like an old man. One of Mandela's household chores was to iron Jongintaba's trousers, which he performed without complaint. When he grew up, Mandela followed Jongintaba's example, always taking great pride in his appearance and dress.

beautiful gardens, fruit trees, and fields. He had never seen such a magnificent home—two rectangular buildings and seven rondavels (round dwellings), all with floorboards, the first Nelson had ever seen. Nelson was delighted to learn he would live here and be treated as one of Jongintaba's children.

A compound of rondavels in Mvezo

Nelson adapted quickly. He missed Qunu and his mother, but he enjoyed the company of the other children—Justice (Jongintaba's son), Nomafu (Jongintaba's daughter), Sabata (Jongintaba's young half-brother and the future king), and Nxeko (Sabata's brother). Nelson attended the schoolhouse next to the palace and applied himself to his English studies. When not in school, Nelson played outside, tending sheep and riding horses.

Although baptized in Qunu, Nelson had not attended church, but here, in Mqhekezweni, he accompanied Jongintaba and his wife to church. Fiery preaching, joyful singing, and fervent prayers became part of his Sunday routine.

Nelson also attended the tribal meetings over which Jongintaba presided. Thembu men—farmers, laborers, shopkeepers—traveled to the palace on horse or by foot to discuss issues related to cattle, droughts, and policies instituted by the British. The Thembu regent let everyone speak and he listened to all—even to those who were most critical. After everyone had a chance to speak Jongintaba, a highly skilled leader, summarized what he had heard and sought consensus. Nelson, who was being groomed to counsel the tribal rulers—as his father Chief Henry had been—learned by example.

To prepare Nelson for his role as counselor to the king, Jongintaba arranged for Nelson to attend Clarkebury Boarding Institute, a Methodist school built in the colonial style on the other side of the Mbashe River. Nelson was proud of the shiny pair of boots Jongintaba gave him to mark the occasion—pleased also to arrive at his new school in a Ford motor car driven by the regent.

Nelson had never worn boots before—at first, they made so much noise that other students teased him. His embarrassment, however, did not last long, and he adapted well to the new school. He became fond of Reverend Cecil Harris, the seemingly stern head of school, and of his wife and children—the first white family he had ever known.

Both Jongintaba and Justice had attended the school so Nelson expected to receive special treatment, but to his surprise he did not. Many of the students were both brighter and more athletic; still, Nelson was a hard worker and finished the three-year course of study in two.

Nelson moved on to Healdtown, a large Methodist mission college with ivy-covered buildings. Situated in Fort Beaufort almost two hundred miles to the southwest, the college attracted more than one thousand students from various tribes and different parts of the country. Once again Nelson was exposed to British culture, its history, and government. As a dorm prefect he became responsible for supervising other students. For recreation he took up long-distance running as well as boxing.

While at Healdtown, Nelson heard Krune Mqhayi, a Xhosa poet, talk of "the brutal clash between what is indigenous and good, and what is foreign and bad." Nelson considered this a bold statement and was shocked to hear criticism of the British. At the same time he started to question many of his own assumptions—and he began to look at the Afrikaner and the British with a more discerning eye.

It was in 1935 that Nelson attended the initiation school at Tyhalarha, on the banks of the Mbashe River. During an elaborate ceremony that followed the circumcision, the initiates were given gifts—two heifers and four sheep for Nelson, along with a new name: Dalibunga. "I remember walking differently on that day, straighter, taller, firmer," Mandela later wrote. "I was hopeful, and thinking that I might some day have wealth, property and status."

The initiates also feasted and listened to praise songs and speeches. One speaker, the king's brother, Chief Meligqili, congratulated the youth for embracing their Xhosa traditions. But then in the presence of all—family members, chiefs, counselors, and the regents—Chief Meligquili changed his tone:

> There sit our sons, young, healthy, and handsome, the flower of the Xhosa tribe, the pride of our nation. We have just circumcised them in a ritual that promises their manhood, but I am here to tell you that it is an empty, illusory promise, a promise that can never be fulfilled. For we Xhosa, and

all black South Africans, are a conquered people. We are slaves in our own country. We are tenants on our own soil. We have no strength, no power, no control over our own destiny in the land of our birth. . . . The abilities, the intelligence, the promise of these young men will be squandered in their attempt to eke out a living doing the simplest most mindless chores for the white man. These gifts today are naught, for we cannot give them the greatest gift of all, which is freedom and independence.

At the time Nelson did not feel oppressed; only later would he remember the chief's words and know that they were true.

Initiates dressed in palm leaf skirts, head and face gear dance at a circumcision ceremony in the Transkei, circa 1925.

The Seeds of White Rule

The beginnings of white rule in South Africa began in 1652, with the arrival of Dutch settlers. They came on an expedition led by Jan van Riebeek, a merchant who represented the Dutch East India Company, which had sent him to establish a trading station between Amsterdam and the Dutch East Indies at Table Bay (now Cape Town). It was not long after the arrival of van Riebeek and his crew that they were followed by other Dutch settlers, French Calvinists, and Germans. In 1756 the settlers began importing slaves from Malaysia, Madagascar, India, Indonesia, Mozambique, and East Africa. Van Riebeek owned eighteen slaves.

Early on, the settlers began migrating into areas occupied by the indigenous peoples, the Stone Age San and the Khoikhoi, who had inhabited the Cape regions from at least 2000 BCE. By the end of the seventeenth century, Dutch settlers were farming far beyond the original boundaries of the Cape.

In 1795, British forces seized control of the Cape colony—soon many citizens of the English Isles began immigrating to South Africa. The colony steadily grew and prospered. But the descendants of the early Dutch settlers, who became known as Afrikaners, resented the British. Dutch farmers, or *trekboers*, migrated away from the Cape region to lands not yet colonized

Jan van Riebeeck arriving in Table Bay in 1652, as depicted in a painting by Charles Davidson Bell, who lived from 1813 to 1882.

by Europeans. Traveling on horseback and in wagons, their search for new lands pitted them against the Xhosa and other tribes. From the start, the settlers considered themselves superior, particularly the Calvinist Boers, who believed that Africans were subhuman and predestined for hell by God. A white visitor to the region noted, "They (the whites) call themselves people and Christians, and the Kaffirs and the Hottentots heathens, and on the strength of this they consider themselves entitled to anything." (Kaffir and Hottentot are pejoratives.)

Boer guerrillas during the Second Boer War

The first major clash between the *trekboers* and the Xhosa took place in 1702. The Xhosa were no match against the Boers, who were heavily armed with shotguns. Without water and grazing land for their cattle and sheep, the Xhosa had no choice but to work on Boer farms to support their families.

Tensions between the British and Boers continued to escalate, especially after the Empire abolished slavery in 1834, and gold and diamonds were discovered on tribal lands. The Boers, meanwhile, had claimed for themselves rural areas in the nothern regions of Southern Africa. They named these areas the Transvaal and the Orange Free state; together, the provinces became known as the South African Republic (SAR). As far as the Boers were concerned, the British, native Africans, and all other groups not of Dutch origin had no political rights in the Boer-controlled SAR; all were considered "foreigners." This led to Anglo Boer wars between 1899 and 1902.

The bitter wars ended in May 1902. The Boers lost to the British, and the Union of South Africa came into being in 1909, concentrating power in an all-white parliament. The British then created the South African Native Affairs Commission, which proposed racial segregation in the areas of land, labor, education, and politics.

After leaving Healdtown, Nelson attended the University College of Fort Hare—the only black university in South Africa and home to many African scholars. For the start of his new university life, Jongintaba took Nelson to a tailor and had a three-piece suit made for him.

At Fort Hare, Nelson broadened his horizons, studying anthropology, Roman Dutch law, politics, and native administration. He also took up soccer, ballroom dancing, and drama, acting as John Wilkes Booth in a play about Abraham Lincoln. He joined the Southern Christian Association and taught Sunday school classes. He taught bible classes on Sunday with one of his soccer teammates, Oliver Tambo. Oliver was a brilliant science student and a skilled debater who would prove to be a lifelong friend and Nelson's partner in the great liberation struggle to come. He also became best friends with Kaiser Matanzima. Matanzima was Mandela's nephew from the Thembu Royal family, but Matanzima was older than Nelson. "The two of us were very handsome young men," Matanzima recalled, "and all the women wanted us. . . . We were always together: when someone saw me alone, they would say, 'Where's Nelson?' . . . We had warm hearts together."

After two years Nelson was nominated to stand for election to the Student Representative Council. Students threatened to boycott the elections unless student representatives were allowed to play a greater role in the administration of the school—they also wanted more and better campus food. After visiting whites-only Rhodes University for sporting contests and debates, students at Fort Hare realized their meals were terrible and sparse. With only a quarter of the students voting, Nelson and five others were elected. The six elected representatives voted unanimously to support the boycott and refused to take on their elected positions.

Dr. Alexander Kerr, the principal, accepted their resignations and called for new elections the following evening during supper when all students would be in attendance. Yet again only a small number of students voted—and the same six students were elected. Five agreed to serve; Nelson, however, refused, choosing to support the boycott instead.

Nelson met with Dr. Kerr and explained his decision. Dr. Kerr told Nelson he would have to expel him if he refused to participate. He would let Nelson take a day to reconsider.

Nelson wanted very much to graduate. He reminded himself that with a BA degree he could become successful, find useful employment, and earn enough money to buy a house for his mother. But Nelson also wanted to stand by his principles. Still unsure, he met with Dr. Kerr the following morning. On the spot he decided he could not serve. "This was one of my first battles with authority," Mandela later recalled, "and I felt the sense of power that comes from having right and justice on one's side."

Dr. Alexander Kerr

Dr. Kerr was disappointed—yet he would give Nelson one more chance. If Nelson agreed to join the Student Representative Council, he would allow Nelson to return after the summer break.

Nelson spent the summer in Mqhekezweni with Jonginbata. The regent was appalled to hear what had transpired and insisted Nelson return to the university. Under no circumstances did he want Nelson to jeopardize his education or his future.

Jongintaba expected Nelson to follow his advice not only in regards to his academic future, but in all other respects—including matrimony. Eager to see both Nelson and Justice married before he died, Jongintaba chose the daughter of a Thembu nobleman for

Justice and the daughter of a Thembu priest for Nelson. Jongintaba also arranged for the lobola, a dowry of cattle to be paid to the families of both brides.

The regent was following Thembu custom in selecting brides for his sons, but Nelson wanted no part of it. He was not ready to marry and did not favor Jongintaba's choice. What's more, the girl was "very, very ugly," as one relative recalled, and Jongintaba was not aware of an affair between Justice and the girl. "[Nelson] feared to tell his father the truth that the lady . . . [was], in actual fact, in love with [his] cousin brother [Justice]."

Nelson's future looked bleak. Jongintaba, a generous man who had become a father to him, was demanding that he make compromises he had no desire to make. The consequences would be long-term. Justice too was not prepared to do his father's bidding. The two young men deliberated. Nelson had always felt gratitude for all that Jongintaba had done for him, but he needed the freedom to make his own decisions. If Jongintaba could not be dissuaded, his only recourse would be to run away. Justice was prepared to accompany him.

Nineteen-year-old Mandela wearing his first suit, which was bought by Jongintaba

Later in life, Mandela often reflected on the formative years he spent with Chief Jongintaba and his wife No-England (right). He recalled the Ford in which Jongintaba drove him to Clarkebury (top photo). And he praised Jongintaba's leadership style, with its emphasis on persuasion and consensus. Below: In this 1930 photo, nine horsemen travel to meet with Jongintaba.

What's in a Name?

By the time he was sixteen, Mandela had three different names, and today he is known by even more: Rolihlahla, Nelson, Dalibhunga, Madiba, Tata, and Khulu.

Rolihlahla, his birth name, literally means in the Xhosa language "pulling the branch of a tree," but colloquially it means "troublemaker." In the indigenous isiXhosa alphabet "r" does not stand alone; it is always "rh." Nevertheless, in his autobiography, Mandela wrote his name as Rolihlahla. The name was given by his father, and it is pronounced as,

R oh - L ee - SL ah - SL ah where,

R	is pronounced as	r	in rat
oh	is pronounced as	o	in so
L	is pronounced as	l	in let
ee	is pronounced as	ee	in see
SL	is pronounced as	sl	in slam
ah	is pronounced as	a	in car
SL	is pronounced as	sl	in slate
ah	is pronounced as	a	in car

Mandela – This name comes from Chief Henry's side of the family. Chief Henry's great-grandfather was King Ngubengcuka, who united the Thembu before colonization by the British. King Ngubengcuka had a son named Mandela, and he became Nelson's grandfather.

Nelson – This name was given to him on his first day at school by his teacher, Miss Mdingane. Giving African children English names was a custom among Africans in the early twentieth century, and was influenced by British colonials who could not easily, and often would not, pronounce African names. It is unclear why Miss Mdingane chose the name "Nelson."

Dalibhunga – This is the name given to Mandela at the age of sixteen after he had undergone initiation, the traditional Xhosa rite of passage into manhood. It means "creator or founder of the council" or "convenor of the dialogue." According to a relative, Chief N. Mtirara, "each and every chief or prince in accordance with our custom, after circumcision, he is given a praise name, so that his original first name, like that one of Rolihlahla is no longer used. Instead of it, he is being called Chief Dalibhunga."

Madiba – This is the name of the clan of which Mandela is a member. A clan name is much more important than a surname as it refers to the ancestor from which a person is descended. Madiba was the name of a Thembu chief who ruled in the Transkei in the eighteenth century. It is considered very polite to use someone's clan name.

Tata – This means "father" and is a term of endearment. Mandela is a father figure to many, and anyone, regardless of age, can call him Tata.

Khulu – "Khulu" means great, paramount, grand. When referring to Mandela as "Khulu," the speaker means "Great One." It is also a shortened form of the isiXhosa word "uBawomkhulu" for "grandfather."

TWO

"Bound Heart and Soul"

Justice and Nelson made preparations for their escape—selling two of the family's oxen so they could pay for train tickets. The young men hired a car to take them to the train station—but the station manager told them he was under strict orders from Jongintaba not to sell them tickets. (Jongintaba must have suspected they would run away and called ahead to the station manager.) Nelson and Justice rushed to the train station in the next town—hoping to find better luck there.

This time their ticket purchase did not arouse suspicion. They traveled to Queenstown where they planned to procure the necessary documents to continue on to Johannesburg. A relative introduced them to the local magistrate who could provide the travel permits. Nelson and Justice told him they needed to go to Johannesburg to conduct business for the regent. The magistrate decided to check with his colleague in Umtata, Jongintaba's home district, before handing over the documents to the boys. But as luck would have it, Jongintaba was visiting the Umtata magistrate when he received the phone call from the Queenstown magistrate. Jongintaba insisted on having the boys arrested.

The Queenstown magistrate was furious—he did not like being deceived. The boys pleaded with him not to arrest them. Nelson explained that they had lied—but they had not broken the law.

They could not be arrested simply because their father wanted it so. Reluctantly the magistrate let them go.

Justice and Nelson decided to risk crossing into Johannesburg without permits (called "passes"). An old friend in Queenstown found someone to give them a ride to Johannesburg in return for fifteen pounds sterling—a considerable sum which left them almost penniless. The first sight of Johannesburg—bright lights, tall buildings, and billboards advertising candy, cigarettes, and beer—took them by surprise. No one stopped them to ask for their passes. To their delight they spent the night in the servants' quarters of a beautiful grand home in a suburb of Johannesburg.

Pass Laws

South Africa had a law known as the 1923 Natives [Urban Areas] Act, and it designated urban areas in South Africa as "white." All black men and women in cities and towns had to carry special papers called "passes" at all times. Anyone caught without a pass would be arrested immediately and sent to a rural area, which is why Mandela and Justice found traveling to Johannesburg risky and difficult. The Natives [Urban Areas] Act was one in a long series of acts designed to segregate the population in South Africa. In 1913, the Natives Land Act had forced black South Africans to live on 7.3 percent of the country's land (extended to 13 percent in 1936)—though Africans made up 80 percent of the population. Africans were allowed to be on "white" land only if they were working for whites.

Then, in 1952, came the Pass Laws Act, making it mandatory for *all* black South Africans over the age of sixteen to carry a "pass book" at all times. The law stipulated where, when, and for how long a person could remain in an area. Also known as a *dompas*, the document contained a person's fingerprints, photograph, the name of his/her employer, his/her address, the length of employment, and other identification information. Under the law only whites could be employers.

Later Jongintaba became resigned to the boys living in Johannesburg. With the help of his father, Justice found a job as a clerk at Crown Mines, the largest gold mine in the area. The year was 1941. Justice arranged for Mandela to work as a night watchman. But, after only a few days, Jongintaba learned that Mandela had boasted about deceiving the regent and running away. He sent a telegram to the head of the mines with the words, "SEND BOYS HOME AT ONCE."

Justice and Nelson lost their jobs at the mines—but they did not return home. Mandela had decided to become a lawyer and planned to stay in the city with his cousin Garlick Mbekeni. Mandela wanted to take correspondence classes at the University of South Africa to finish his bachelor of arts degree and then study law. His cousin arranged for Nelson to meet his good friend Walter Sisulu—a businessman and community leader who ran a real estate company. Raised by his mother and uncle in the Transkei, Sisulu had moved to Johannesburg. He worked in a gold mine and later in a bank before starting his own real estate company.

Sisulu took a keen interest in Mandela. He introduced him to a white lawyer named Lazar Sidelsky who handled mortgages for many African clients. Mandela was offered a job as a clerk in the Witkin, Sidelksy and Eidelman law firm. Principals in the firm encouraged Mandela to continue his education so that he could become an "articled" clerk—a prerequisite to becoming an attorney.

The staff at Witkin, Sidelksy and Eidelman insisted they had no color bar. But Mandela and Gaur Radebe, the only other black employee, discovered otherwise when one of the secretaries served tea. She had purchased two new cups and expected Mandela and Radebe to drink only from those. Radebe refused to follow the instructions and drank from one of the cups reserved for whites. Mandela was less willing to make a scene but did not want to disappoint Radebe. He turned down the tea altogether.

Mandela soon made his first white friend—an articled clerk at the firm named Nat Bregman, a cousin of Sidelsky and a member of the Communist Party. Bregman took him to get-togethers where he socialized with people of different races—Africans, whites, Indians, and Coloureds. They discussed Communist philosophy, and Mandela was struck by the emphasis Bregman placed on sharing wealth. For Bregman and his party the struggle focused on class—"the haves" and "the have-nots."

A view of Johannesburg in 1938

Mandela found a room to rent in Alexandra township, a crowded yet vibrant slum known as "Dark City." He felt at home there and scraped by with very little money—reading by candlelight because he could not afford a kerosene lamp. He walked to work to save bus fare. He economized on food and wore the same suit every day—a hand-me-down from Lazar Sidelsky, who had practically become "an elder brother" to Mandela. "It was hard going and I often found it quite difficult to pay the rent and bus fare," Mandela later wrote. "But my landlord and his wife were kind, not only did they give me an extension when I could not raise the rent, but on Sundays they gave me a lovely lunch free of charge."

At the end of Mandela's first year in Johannesburg, the regent paid him a visit. He saw that Mandela had moved on with his life. Much to Mandela's relief, Jongintaba showed no anger towards Mandela. He was prepared to forgive Mandela for running away— leaving behind Fort Hare and abandoning marriage plans. The regent did urge Justice to return home—Justice, after all, would need to prepare for his new role as a chief. Justice, however, was still unwilling to return.

Six months after this visit took place, the regent died. Mandela and Justice traveled back to the Transkei for the funeral but missed it by a day. Mandela mourned the loss of the father figure he had grown to love. He had come to respect Jongintaba for his leadership qualities—his tolerance and his ability to unite people with different views. Justice was expected to become chief, and he chose to remain in Mqhekezweni to take on his new position. But Mandela stayed only a week—the Thembu village had lost its appeal. The big city was now far more attractive.

Meanwhile, Great Britain had declared war on Germany. South African prime minister Barry Herzog wanted his country

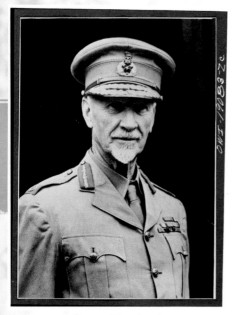
General Jan Smuts

to remain neutral; he was deposed and replaced by General Jan Smuts, who had previously served as prime minister from 1919 to 1924. The Union of South Africa entered the war in September 1939—siding with Great Britain against Germany and the Axis powers.

Mandela watched as the world events unfolded—well aware that the decisions impacting Africans were made not by Africans, but by white people. He moved into a compound in downtown Johannesburg with neighbors from a wide range of tribes and countries—Sothos, Zulus, Swazis, Xhosas, Namibians, and Mozambicans—and he gained a new appreciation of their common bond. He did not need to be reminded of the richness of African culture. Every day he heard multiple languages.

In 1942, Mandela passed the final exams for his bachelor of arts degree. With his new degree, he hoped he could become an articled clerk, but his friend Radebe—already an articled clerk—explained that the firm only needed one black articled clerk to bring in clients from the black community. Although the principals of the law firm would never admit it, they would not article a second black man. If Radebe were to leave, however, Mandela's future was assured. Radebe's analysis would prove correct. When Radebe left the following year to start his own firm, Mandela became an articled clerk.

Radebe, a man of deep commitment to the African freedom struggle, was influential in other ways as well—introducing Nelson to members of the African National Congress (ANC).

Founded in 1912, this organization sought to unite Africans, give them a voice in parliament, and increase education and business opportunities. The ANC had designed a flag with three colors—black for the people, green for the land, and gold for the country's resources. Their anthem *"Nkosi Sikelel' iAfrika"* (Lord Bless Africa) was written by a Xhosa composer, Enoch Sontonga.

At first Mandela said little at ANC meetings—he preferred to listen. But, slowly, he began to form his own opinions and take part. In August 1943, the ANC organized

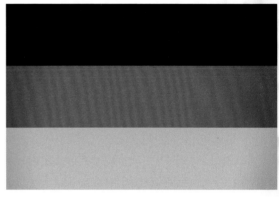

The ANC flag

a bus boycott in Alexandra to protest a fare increase from four to five pence. Ten thousand men and women participated—and Mandela was one of them. After nine days, the boycott, which Radebe had helped lead, proved successful. The bus company retained the four-pence fare.

The boycott marked a turning point in Mandela's life. Before the protest he had measured his own achievements by what he could provide for his family, but now his perspective changed—he wanted to improve conditions for all black South Africans. More acutely aware of racial oppression and the lack of opportunities for Africans, he was also more determined to speak out.

Mandela remained at the law firm while enrolling at the University of the Witswatersrand to study for a law degree—the only black to do so. His classmates had mixed reactions. Some were decidedly hostile, but others were more open-minded. Mandela made friends with Indian and white students, men and women devoted to the freedom struggle, among them Joe Slovo and Ruth First, both children of Jewish immigrants and members of the Communist Party.

Walter Sisulu and his wife, Albertina, a nurse at Johannesburg General Hospital, encouraged Mandela to visit their home frequently. They spent long hours discussing politics and sharing meals. Mandela came to admire Walter's intellect and good sense. "He never lost his head in a crisis; he was often silent when others were shouting." Through Walter, Mandela also met Anton Muziwakhe Lembede, a twenty-nine-year-old Zulu lawyer who urged members of the young, black elite to guard against adopting British culture and manners. Lembede believed that Africans needed to develop a collective and aggressive sense of self worth, and a deep pride in Africa. He wrote:

> Africa is a black man's country. Africans are the natives of Africa and they have inhabited Africa, their Motherland, from times immemorial; Africa belongs to them. Africans are one. . . . The basis of national unity is the nationalistic feeling of the Africans, the feeling of being Africans irrespective of tribal connection, social status, educational attainment, or economic class. . . . My soul yearns for the glory of an Africa that is gone, but I shall labor for the birth of a new Africa, free and great among the nations of the world.

Mandela believed Anton Lembede was destined to become a leader.

Albertina Sisulu introduced Nelson to Evelyn Mase, Sisulu's younger cousin, who worked with Albertina at the hospital and was in training to become a nurse. Evelyn had become like a daughter to the Sisulus. She was quiet, reserved, and gracious. "Within days of our first meeting, we were going steady," Evelyn recalled. "I think I loved him the first time I saw him. There was something very special about Nelson."

Walter and Albertina Sisulu on their wedding day in 1944. On the left is best man Nelson Mandela and bridesmaid Evelyn Mase (left of Walter), whom he later married.

Mandela and Evelyn quickly fell in love and became engaged. In 1944, they married in a civil ceremony to avoid the expense of a traditional wedding. They lived for a short time with Albertina's brother and then moved into their own place in Orlando, a black township located twelve miles outside of Johannesburg. (This township had been planned in the 1930s by the white government for "the better class of native.") The couple was "allocated a two-roomed house," which typically had no floor and no ceiling. The roads between the houses were dirt tracks. Nevertheless, it was the first home Mandela could call his own.

A son, named Thembikile, was born in 1946. Nelson took great pleasure in caring for the baby whenever he could, but he was often away from home. A year later a daughter, Makaziwe, was born. Both Evelyn and Mandela worried about Makaziwe's poor health. She grew more frail and died at nine months. "We were heart-broken," said Evelyn.

Mandela discussed political ideas with Sisulu and Lembede, as well as Oliver Tambo, his friend from Fort Hare. Eager for the ANC to take a more active role, they formed a branch composed of younger members—the Youth League. Mandela was chosen to serve on the executive committee; Lembede was elected president, Tambo secretary, and Sisulu treasurer. Their goals were far-reaching—they wanted to bring together Africans from many tribes, unite them in the freedom struggle, abolish white supremacy, and establish a democratic government. The Youth League drew attention to oppressive laws that took away the rights of black people so that they could not own land, vote, or work in a skilled trade. Their manifesto called for the end to white domination, the rejection of foreign leadership, and the national liberation of Africans.

In 1946, the Asiatic Land Tenure Act (often referred to as the Ghetto Act) gave Indians in South Africa minimal political representation, but restricted the rights of Indians to live in certain areas and to buy or lease land. Indentured laborers from India had lived in South Africa for decades. The first to arrive came in 1860, recruited by British colonists to cut sugarcane on their plantations in the South African province of Natal. Between 1860 and 1911, when indentures stopped, as many as 152,000 Indians had landed in South Africa, and more than half (52 percent) had decided to remain after serving out their contracts. By 1946, roughly 500,000 lived in the country.

The Natal Indian Congress, an organization of Indians devoted to promoting the rights of Indians in South Africa, mounted a protest campaign. For two years they marched, picketed, and held rallies; many were sent to jail. They were inspired by Mohandas

Gandhi, a leader in the formation of this congress in 1894, who believed one could overcome evil by good. He had advocated the use of nonviolent resistance, which he called satyagraha.

Founders of the Natal Indian Congress in 1895.
Mohandas Gandhi is in the top row, fourth from left.

Impressed by "the meticulous organization" of the Natal Indian Congress, as well as its "willingness to suffer and sacrifice," Mandela urged the ANC to support the Congress. In 1947 he was elected to his first official position in the ANC, becoming a member of the executive committee of the Transvaal ANC. "I was now bound heart and soul," he said. That same year, leaders of the ANC, the Transvaal Indian Congress, and the Natal Indian Congress signed a pact to unite their organizations and solidify their common goals.

Dr. Daniel Malan (front center) and cabinet

In 1948, the National Party and Dr. Daniel Malan, a former minister of the Dutch Reformed Church, won an election in which only whites could vote. The Nationalists, sympathetic to the Nazis, had opposed South Africa's involvement on the side of the Allies in World War II. Once in power, the new all-white government enacted laws to ensure a system of total racial segregation known as apartheid (a word that means "apartness" in Afrikaans).

The Screws
of Segration Tighten

Once in power, the National Party wasted no time passing successive laws to keep the races segregated in South Africa:

1949: The Prohibition of Mixed Marriages banned interracial marriages.

1950: The Population Registration Act forced all South Africans to register by color: African/black, which comprised nine distinct nations (Zulu, Xhosa, Venda, Tsonga, Pedi, Tswana, Swazi, Ndebele, and Sotho); Coloured (mixed black, Malayan, and white descent); Asian (Indian in ancestry); and white—Dutch (Afrikaner/Boer) and British (Anglo descent).

1950: The Immorality Act outlawed all sexual relations beween whites and nonwhites.

1950: The Suppression of Communism Act prohibited any acts or strategies that might promote political, social, or economic changes.

1951: The Group Areas Act set aside specific communities for each of the races. The best areas and the majority of the land were reserved for whites. Non-whites were relocated into "reserves."

1951: The Bantu Homelands Act declared that the lands reserved for black Africans were independent nations. This served to strip millions of blacks of their South African citizenship. Blacks were now considered foreigners in white-controlled South Africa and needed passports to enter these areas. (They could only enter to work for whites in menial jobs.)

1952: The Abolition of Passes and Coordination of Documents Act ended the pass system but required all Africans to carry "reference" books with various forms of identification. From 1948 to 1973, more than 10 million Africans were arrested because their reference books were "not in order." (The name of this act is misleading.)

1953: The Preservation of Separate Amenities Act established separate parks, beaches, post offices, and other public places for whites and nonwhites.

1953: The Bantu Education Act gave the government the right to supervise the education of all blacks.

Many Africans, including Mandela, were surprised to find the Nationalist Party emerge victorious. Although for centuries whites, blacks, Coloureds, and Indians had lived separately, these patterns now became law, deepening the divisions. Racial groups lived in designated areas—whites declared to whom the land belonged. Nonwhites could not attend the same schools or go to the same restaurants, movie theaters, and beaches as whites. They drank from separate water fountains and used separate restrooms. Africans and Indians lost the minimal political representation they had once gained.

A "whites-only" sign from the apartheid era

The ANC redoubled its efforts to bring about change. They organized boycotts, protests, and strikes. Mandela, Sisulu, Tambo, and other members of the Youth League wanted to take more extreme actions. They met with ANC president Alfred Xuma to convince him to stage a campaign that would involve far greater numbers of people. Willing to go to jail if necessary, they modeled their strategy after Gandhi's civil resistance campaigns in South Africa as well as in India.

Xuma refused to consider this new course of action—he believed the timing was not right; the country was not ready. Mandela and other Youth League members supported a new candidate for the ANC presidency, Dr. James S. Moroka. The Youth League was successful: Moroka won the election. The ANC would mount a more vigorous campaign against apartheid, and Nelson Mandela would emerge as a more effective leader, deeply committed to the cause, poised to send a strong message, and eager to insist on immediate change.

three

Freedom Fighter

On May 1, 1950, the Communist Party organized a one-day strike to call for the abolition of discriminatory laws. The National Party reacted strongly—passing a law that made it a crime to belong to the Communist Party and participate in its activities. This law gave the government the right to suppress other groups as well.

"Today it is the Communist Party. Tomorrow it will be our trade unions, our Indian Congress, our APO (African People's Organization whose members were Coloured), our African National Congress," Oliver Tambo said. The passage of the National Party Act prompted the Communist Party to stage a National Day of Protest on June 26, 1950. Mandela had always been reluctant to work with the Communist Party but he now changed course—recognizing that the ANC and the Communist Party shared common goals. As a newly elected member of the ANC's National Executive Committee, he worked with regional leaders to help plan a massive strike throughout the country for the National Day of Protest. The day marked an important milestone in the struggle; in future years "Freedom Day" would be observed on June 26.

After the strike Mandela continued to devote his time to ANC activities; he saw less and less of his family. There were always letters to write, people to see, meetings to attend, trips to make.

In 1951, Walter Sisulu suggested waging a national civil disobedience campaign against the new laws that took away more rights of Africans. A committee of four—two ANC men (Sisulu and J. B. Marks) and two members of the South African Indian Congress (Yusuf Dadoo and Usuf Cachalia)—drafted a letter asking for the repeal of six laws. The letter, or ultimatum, would be signed by Moroka, the ANC president, and Sisulu and addressed to Prime Minister Daniel Malan. The letter spoke of "democracy, liberty and harmony," and it declared that the African people were "fully resolved to achieve this in our lifetime."

Mandela, one of the few blacks to have a driver's license, was asked to deliver the letter. He borrowed a car and drove almost three hundred miles to obtain Moroka's signature. He was stopped by the police and his car was ransacked; nevertheless the police let him proceed, and Moroka approved the letter.

However, Prime Minister Malan stood his ground and refused to concede, reiterating the Nationalist ideology that "Bantu differ in many ways from the Europeans" and that "the government had no intention of repealing . . . the laws." He further made it clear that he would "use the full machinery at its disposal to quell any disturbances."

Mandela and other ANC leaders immediately set about enlisting more volunteers to promote the civil disobedience campaign. A pamphlet distributed by the ANC, in both English and Afrikaans, stated: "we stand on the eve of a great national crisis. We call on every true South African to support us."

For his part, Mandela spoke frequently to various groups to recruit new members. He had become a skilled speaker and easily developed a good rapport with his audience.

Ten thousand people came out to hear Mandela in Durban, a large city on South Africa's Indian Ocean coast. Mandela urged them to join the ANC campaign and focus the attention of the world on the country's racist policies. Although the campaign would be nonviolent, its leaders must be willing to take risks—they could be deported, imprisoned, or shot.

Mandela encouraged young people to take on the government. In an address to the ANC Youth League, he said, "[T]he spirit of the people cannot be crushed, and no matter what happens to the present leadership, new leaders will arise like mushrooms till full victory is won." He added, "Sons and daughters of Africa, our tasks are mighty indeed, but I have abundant faith in our ability to reply to the challenge posed by the situation. Under the slogan of FULL DEMOCRATIC RIGHTS IN SOUTH AFRICA NOW, we must march forward into victory."

On June 26, 1952, the Day of Defiance, as the mass protest became known, started as scheduled. "Defiers" entered areas where access to Africans was routinely denied. Some crossed into a "Whites Only" area at a railroad station and were arrested. Others, led by Sisulu and Nana Sita, an Indian resister, attempted to enter a township near Boksburg without the proper permits. As soon as the police opened the gates the defiers—fifty-two strong—crossed into the forbidden area. They were immediately arrested.

Mandela watched as events unfolded according to plan. After the Boksburg arrest he delivered a letter to the magistrate explaining the actions of the defiers. That evening, he attended a meeting to discuss further acts of defiance. By the time he left it was after 11 p.m. and a curfew was in effect. Mandela had not planned to be detained at this stage of the protest, but he was taken by surprise. The police arrested him and sent him to jail.

Prison conditions were grim—the cells were not sanitary and the warders kicked and shoved. Still the "defiers" joined in the singing of "*Nkosi Sikelel' iAfrika*" ("God Bless Africa")—the song that had become their anthem—and they were soon released. "The camaraderie of our fellow defiers made the two days pass quickly," Mandela later wrote.

The Defiance Campaign was gaining momentum—and Mandela was making a name for himself. A white South African in Durban remarked, "I noticed people turning and staring at the opposite pavement and I saw this magnificent figure of a man, immaculately dressed. Not just blacks, but whites, including white women, were turning to admire him."

Various groups, including Communists, Indians, Coloureds, and Africans, devoted time and energy to the campaign. During the next five months, more than 8,500 protesters were arrested. The Nationalists looked for new ways to discourage demonstrations and strikes. They passed the Public Safety Act, which allowed the government to declare martial law and detain people without trial. The Criminal Laws Amendment legalized corporal punishment for resisters. The government also enforced "banning"—restricting a person to a certain area and prohibiting participation in certain organizations or large gatherings. A banned person who disobeyed orders would be imprisoned.

On July 30, 1952, Mandela was arrested for violation of the Suppression of Communism Act. Nineteen leaders of the freedom struggle were arrested. Among them were Walter Sisulu and Ahmed Kathrada, a member of the South African Indian Congress, who had joined the Young Communist League at the age of twelve.

Schoolchildren and university students took part in the massive demonstrations to protest the arrests. Many of them attended the trial—the courtroom was filled to capacity. On December 2, 1952, Judge Frans Rumpff found Mandela and the other leaders guilty of "statutory communism." Although those arrested were not all members of the Communist Party, they had opposed the government and could therefore be convicted under the Suppression of Communism Act. The judge conceded that although the accused had planned acts of noncompliance, their leaders had advised the volunteers to act nonviolently. He ordered that the accused be imprisoned for nine months with hard labor, a sentence that was later suspended.

Left to right: African National Congress leader J. S. Moroka, Mandela, and Yusuf Dadoo, president of the South African Indian Congress, outside the courthouse during the Defiance Campaign trial

Chief Albert Luthuli was elected president in the 1952 ANC elections. Luthuli was a Zulu chief, a teacher, and the son of a Seventh-Day Adventist minister. The government paid him a stipend as a tribal chief but threatened to dismiss him if he took on the leadership of the ANC. Luthuli would not relinquish his ANC post and had to give up his role as tribal chief. He remained wholly committed to the struggle, devoting his energy to nonviolent resistance.

Mandela was elected first deputy vice-president but, as one of many leaders banned by the government, he could not openly participate in ANC activities. (As a banned person, Mandela could not talk to more than one person at a time, nor was he allowed to attend his own son's birthday party.)

If the government were to declare the ANC illegal, all members—not only those who were banned—would be silenced. Mandela devised a plan to assure that the work of the ANC could continue secretly. This plan, which became known as the M-Plan, was presented to the National Executive Committee of the ANC. It allowed for the organization to communicate with its members and recruit new ones without the government becoming aware of its activities.

Mandela created a structure that included cell stewards (each in charge of ten houses), street stewards (to whom the cell stewards would report), chief stewards, and a secretariat (to whom the chief stewards reported). He also stressed the importance of education—several of the banned members started to give evening lectures on economics and politics, often in people's homes. And, at first, the government suspected nothing.

The M-Plan was met with mixed reaction. Those in the Eastern Cape, to the south of Johannesburg, were most supportive; they welcomed the plot to circumvent the government. Others feared Mandela and the National Executive Committee were trying to wrest power from local ANC organizers.

Mandela's family continued to grow. A second son, Makgatho, was born in 1951, named for a past president of the ANC. A daughter was born in 1954—she was called Makaziwe in memory of his first daughter, who had died as a baby.

In 1952, Mandela and Oliver Tambo, his friend from Fort Hare, formed their own law practice. The two attorneys had no shortage of work. Each day brought a wide range of clients—an African or a Coloured man who had been evicted, losing a home that had been in his family for generations, a medicine man accused of witchcraft, a black man who walked onto a "Whites Only" beach. Sometimes Mandela had to leave Johannesburg to represent a client—on those occasions he had to apply to have his bans lifted. The government usually acquiesced; still, Mandela was constantly reminded of the restrictions under which he was forced to live.

In 1955, the government began to forcibly remove all Africans from Sophiatown, an area once described as the "Chicago of South Africa" because of its creative community of leading journalists, musicians, writers, and politicians. Sophiatown was unique: there was no municipal ordinance, no superintendent, no wire fences. No permission was needed for Africans to live in Sophiatown. Here, since the early part of the century, blacks, Coloureds, Indians, and Chinese had formed a community.

The Nationalists hated Sophiatown and decided Africans must move thirteen miles to a place called Meadowlands. The ANC opposed the move and staged large demonstrations. On February 10, 1955, the government sent in 2,000 police officers armed with

Black residents of Sophiatown had planned to protest their removals by staging a one-day work stoppage on February 12, 1955, the day on which the removals were due to start. However, the government learned of the plan and sent in 2,000 armed police on February 10. With no means to defend themselves, the first 110 families reluctantly moved to Meadowlands.

machine guns, rifles, and knobkerries. When Sophiatown was finally bulldozed, Father Trevor Huddleston, the Anglican priest of Sophiatown and a fierce critic of racial segregation, said South Africa had lost "not only a place but an ideal."

As the struggle wore on, Mandela's attitude towards the use of nonviolence was changing. He believed that what Gandhi had achieved in India could not be replicated in South Africa. More aggressive tactics were needed. The Nationalists had resorted to violence—the ANC would have to respond in kind. The National Executive Committee of the ANC reprimanded Mandela: They still strictly adhered to a policy of nonviolence. But, as time passed, Mandela became even more adamant that the use of force would be necessary: "A freedom fighter learns the hard way that it is the oppressor who defines the nature of the struggle, and the one oppressed is often left no recourse but to use methods that mirror those of the oppressor. At a certain point, one can only fight fire with fire," he explained.

Although many ANC leaders remained committed to nonviolence, Mandela succeeded in persuading Walter Sisulu to change course. When Sisulu was invited to attend the World Festival of Youth and Students for Peace and Friendship in Bucharest, Mandela suggested he extend his journey. He wanted Sisulu to visit the People's Republic of China and ask for the country's help in procuring arms. Sisulu did so, and he found the Chinese to be sympathetic to the freedom struggle. However, they refused to provide weapons.

The police were becoming more wary of Mandela's role and sought a way to curtail his activities. In September 1953, after his bans had been lifted, Mandela was driving to the town of Villiers in the Orange Free State, seventy-five miles south of Johannesburg, to meet with a client. He expected his presence in the small remote town to go unnoticed, but the police surprised him. He was apprehended and, under the Suppression of Communism Act, ordered to resign from the ANC. Once again he was banned. However, Mandela did not resign from the ANC and continued to engage in secret activities.

Although Mandela could not deliver speeches publicly he continued to write them and have them read aloud. As they were always well received his reputation grew. After he was elected ANC president of the Transvaal (the northern area of the country that includes Johannesburg), he wrote what would become known as "The No Easy Walk to Freedom" speech. It was read on his behalf on September 21, 1953.

Mandela called for new forms of political struggle that were needed to replace the old "suicidal" ways. He described "the grinding poverty of the people, the low wages, the acute shortage of land, the inhuman exploitation and the whole policy of white domination." Living conditions had become "unbearable"—the average family could no longer afford the price of bread. Mandela urged parents to defend their right to play a part in their children's education, and he condemned "the shameful misdeeds of those who rule the country." Drawing to a close, he adapted words spoken by the Indian leader Jawaharlal Nehru, "You can see that 'there is no easy walk to freedom anywhere, and many of us will have to pass through the valley of the shadow of death again and again before we reach the mountain tops of our desires.'"

As word of Mandela's work on behalf of the ANC spread, the Law Society of the Transvaal called for Mandela to lose his license to practice law. Several prominent attorneys, including Afrikaners, volunteered to represent him—at no cost. The judge, an Afrikaner, ruled in favor of Mandela—he would not allow Mandela's political beliefs and actions to stand in the way of his right to practice law. His legal costs would have to be covered by the Law Society.

Yet, at the same time, the National Party was passing laws that would make the life of black people more marginalized—stripping them not only of their rights and land, but of their schools. The

Bantu Education Act allowed the government to oversee a segregated system that offered black children an inferior education. The act also gradually reduced the subsidies given to the country's 4,500 African mission schools. Hendrik Verwoerd, the minister of native affairs, said: "There is no place for [the African] in the European community above the level of certain forms of labour. . . . The school must equip the Bantu to meet the demands which the economic life . . . will impose on him. . . . What is the use of teaching a Bantu child mathematics when it cannot use it in practice?"

Apartheid's Chief Architect

Hendrik Frensch Verwoerd

Hendrik Frensch Verwoerd, a Hollander by birth, is considered the chief architect of apartheid as well as what he later called his "separate nations" theory. Verwoerd was age two when his father brought him to South Africa in 1903. His father moved the family to neighboring Rhodesia (now Zimbabwe) ten years later. Verwoerd earned his master's and doctorate degrees from universities in South Africa, but then continued studying psychology in Germany, where the rise of Nazism was beginning. As minister of native affairs in South Africa (1950-1958) and later as prime minister (1958-1966), Verwoerd aggressively and successfully pushed for the implementation of laws to completely separate the races, such as the Bantu Education Act. Mandela, writing from prison, accused the Nationalists of fascism. "The Nationalist Government has frequently denied that it is a fascist Government inspired by the theories of the National-Socialist Party of Hitlerite Germany. Yet the declarations it makes, the laws it passes and the entire policy it pursues clearly confirm this point." Verwoerd was assassinated by a deranged knifeman in 1966.

The Bantu Education Act stipulated that schools were to be run by the state—only Africans who could afford the fees would be allowed to attend. Most of the churches, with the exception of the Roman Catholics, the Seventh Day Adventists, and the United Jewish Reform Congregation, let the government take over the schools. Unauthorized education was made illegal; those who disobeyed the new law would be fined or imprisoned. The ANC tried to fight back—they organized a boycott and encouraged parents to home-school their children. But their efforts did little to change the school system.

Restrictions were placed on higher education, and educational opportunities were curtailed. The state took control of the only black university in South Africa, the University College of Fort Hare, which Mandela had attended. It also became illegal for non-white students to attend traditionally white universities.

In August 1953, ANC leader Z. K. Matthews proposed that a national conference, representing all groups, be called to "draw up a freedom charter for the democratic South Africa of the future." They created a new body, the National Action Council, which later became known as the Congress Alliance. The Council began planning a Congress of the People for June 25 and 26, 1955. Its goal was to draw up a document that truly represented the political aspirations of all South Africans.

Thousands of written or dictated submissions poured in from hundreds of organizations, and the result was the Freedom Charter. Mandela was part of the committee of the National Action Council that reviewed the final draft.

Black, Coloured, Indian, and white delegates from all over South Africa attended the meeting of the Congress of the People on June 25, 1955, in a private field in Kliptown, near Soweto. Getting there was not easy; police stopped and arrested many because they did not have transport permits.

Mandela was present—but in disguise—when the crowd, 3,000 strong, stood to adopt the Freedom Charter by acclamation. The words resonated throughout the crowd: "South Africa belongs to all who live in it, black and white. . . . no government can justly claim authority unless it is based on the will of the people . . . [E]very man and woman shall have the right to vote for and stand as a candidate for all bodies which make laws."

On the second day, with two sections of the charter still to be discussed, the police arrived in force. Heavily armed, they mounted the platform and announced that they suspected treason was being committed and that the names and addresses of all the delegates would be recorded. Then they began to confiscate documents, posters, and banners. At 8 p.m., the police were still taking down names and addresses as people filed out. The delegates took with them whatever documents and film they could hide.

Black, Coloured, Indian, and white delegates from all over South Africa attended the meeting of the Congress of the People on June 25, 1955, in a private field in Kliptown, near Soweto.

The Freedom Charter

As adopted at the Congress of the People, Kliptown, on 26 June 1955

We, the People of South Africa, declare for all our country and the world to know:

that South Africa belongs to all who live in it, black and white, and that no government can justly claim authority unless it is based on the will of all the people;

that our people have been robbed of their birthright to land, liberty and peace by a form of government founded on injustice and inequality;

that our country will never be prosperous or free until all our people live in brotherhood, enjoying equal rights and opportunities;

that only a democratic state, based on the will of all the people, can secure to all their birthright without distinction of colour, race, sex or belief;

And therefore, we, the people of South Africa, black and white together equals, countrymen and brothers adopt this Freedom Charter;

And we pledge ourselves to strive together, sparing neither strength nor courage, until the democratic changes here set out have been won.

The People Shall Govern!

Every man and woman shall have the right to vote for and to stand as a candidate for all bodies which make laws;

All people shall be entitled to take part in the administration of the country;

The rights of the people shall be the same, regardless of race, colour or sex;

All bodies of minority rule, advisory boards, councils and authorities shall be replaced by democratic organs of self-government.

All National Groups Shall have Equal Rights!

There shall be equal status in the bodies of state, in the courts and in the schools for all national groups and races;

All people shall have equal right to use their own languages, and to develop their own folk culture and customs;

All national groups shall be protected by law against insults to their race and national pride;

The preaching and practice of national, race or colour discrimination and contempt shall be a punishable crime;

All apartheid laws and practices shall be set aside.

The People Shall Share in the Country's Wealth!

The national wealth of our country, the heritage of South Africans, shall be restored to the people;

The mineral wealth beneath the soil, the Banks and monopoly industry shall be transferred to the ownership of the people as a whole;

All other industry and trade shall be controlled to assist the well-being of the people;

All people shall have equal rights to trade where they choose, to manufacture and to enter all trades, crafts and professions.

The Land Shall be Shared Among Those Who Work It!

Restrictions of land ownership on a racial basis shall be ended, and all the land re-divided amongst those who work it to banish famine and land hunger;

The state shall help the peasants with implements, seed, tractors and dams to save the soil and assist the tillers;

Freedom of movement shall be guaranteed to all who work on the land;

All shall have the right to occupy land wherever they choose;

People shall not be robbed of their cattle, and forced labour and farm prisons shall be abolished.

All Shall be Equal Before the Law!

No-one shall be imprisoned, deported or restricted without a fair trial; No one shall be condemned by the order of any Government official;

The courts shall be representative of all the people;

Imprisonment shall be only for serious crimes against the people, and shall aim at re-education, not vengeance;

The police force and army shall be open to all on an equal basis and shall be the helpers and protectors of the people;

All laws which discriminate on grounds of race, colour or belief shall be repealed.

All Shall Enjoy Equal Human Rights!

The law shall guarantee to all their right to speak, to organise, to meet together, to publish, to preach, to worship and to educate their children;

The privacy of the house from police raids shall be protected by law;

All shall be free to travel without restriction from countryside to town, from province to province, and from South Africa abroad;

Pass Laws, permits and all other laws restricting these freedoms shall be abolished.

There Shall be Work and Security!

All who work shall be free to form trade unions, to elect their officers and to make wage agreements with their employers;

The state shall recognise the right and duty of all to work, and to draw full unemployment benefits;

Men and women of all races shall receive equal pay for equal work;

There shall be a forty-hour working week, a national minimum wage, paid annual leave, and sick leave for all workers, and maternity leave on full pay for all working mothers;

Miners, domestic workers, farm workers and civil servants shall have the same rights as all others who work;

Child labour, compound labour, the tot system and contract labour shall be abolished.

The Doors of Learning and Culture Shall be Opened!

The government shall discover, develop and encourage national talent for the enhancement of our cultural life;

All the cultural treasures of mankind shall be open to all, by free exchange of books, ideas and contact with other lands;

The aim of education shall be to teach the youth to love their people and their culture, to honour human brotherhood, liberty and peace;

Education shall be free, compulsory, universal and equal for all children; Higher education and technical training shall be opened to all by means of state allowances and scholarships awarded on the basis of merit;

Adult illiteracy shall be ended by a mass state education plan;

Teachers shall have all the rights of other citizens;

The colour bar in cultural life, in sport and in education shall be abolished.

There Shall be Houses, Security and Comfort!

All people shall have the right to live where they choose, be decently housed, and to bring up their families in comfort and security;

Unused housing space to be made available to the people;

Rent and prices shall be lowered, food plentiful and no-one shall go hungry;

A preventive health scheme shall be run by the state;

Free medical care and hospitalisation shall be provided for all, with special care for mothers and young children;

Slums shall be demolished, and new suburbs built where all have transport, roads, lighting, playing fields, creches and social centres;

The aged, the orphans, the disabled and the sick shall be cared for by the state;

Rest, leisure and recreation shall be the right of all:

Fenced locations and ghettoes shall be abolished, and laws which break up families shall be repealed.

There Shall be Peace and Friendship!

South Africa shall be a fully independent state which respects the rights and sovereignty of all nations;

South Africa shall strive to maintain world peace and the settlement of all international disputes by negotiation—not war;

Peace and friendship amongst all our people shall be secured by upholding the equal rights, opportunities and status of all;

The people of the protectorates Basutoland, Bechuanaland and Swaziland shall be free to decide for themselves their own future;

The right of all peoples of Africa to independence and self-government shall be recognised, and shall be the basis of close co-operation.

Let all people who love their people and their country now say, as we say here:

THESE FREEDOMS WE WILL FIGHT FOR, SIDE BY SIDE, THROUGHOUT OUR LIVES, UNTIL WE HAVE WON OUR LIBERTY

four

On Trial for High Treason

When Mandela's bans expired in September 1955, he traveled to the Transkei to see his family—his "second mother" (the regent's widow) in Mqhekezweni, and his mother and sister in Qunu. His sister Mabel was now married—to the man their sister Baliwe would have married. Baliwe had become engaged only to run away after the *lobola* (dowry) was paid, and Mabel had agreed to marry in her stead.

Mandela very much enjoyed being reunited with his family—spending time with them made him wish for more and he regretted the long distance that separated them. He would have liked to raise his children in the Transkei and live closer to his mother, but he reminded himself that he had made a choice: He was fighting for freedom—it was a decision he did not regret but one that required him to be in Johannesburg. He asked his mother to accompany him to the city. She refused, and Nelson returned without her.

On his way back to Johannesburg, Mandela passed through several forests. He enjoyed the landscape and the animal sightings—the baboons and elephants made a strong impression. "It was ironic that I, an African, was seeing the Africa of storybooks and legend for the first time. Such beautiful land, I thought, and all of it out of reach, owned by whites and untouchable for a black man I could no more choose to live in such beauty than run for Parliament," Mandela wrote.

Mandela did not remain free for long. In March 1956, he was again banned—this time for five years. As before, he continued to work for the ANC while trying not to arouse the suspicions of the government. But state authorities caught wind of Mandela's clandestine activities and were determined to put an end to them.

Early one morning in December of that year, the police arrived at Mandela's home and awoke the family. They produced a warrant for Nelson's arrest, charging him with "high treason." Evelyn and the children watched as the police led him away—they were afraid and had no way of knowing when he would return.

Within a week 156 leaders of the ANC—105 Africans, twenty-one Indians, twenty-three whites, and seven Coloureds—were arrested and taken to the Fort prison in Johannesburg. Among them were Oliver Tambo, Chief Albert Luthuli, and Joe Slovo—a member of the Communist Party and Mandela's former classmate at the University of Witwatersrand.

Upon arrival the men were told to remove their clothes. A doctor inquired about their health. The wardens then gave them permission to dress and divided them into two groups, assigning each group to a cell with one latrine. The conditions were unpleasant, but the prisoners, looking on the bright side, realized they could now talk more freely to each other. Crowded together in tight quarters, they no longer had to make plans to meet secretly. Here no guard monitored their conversation.

The prisoners organized activities—physical exercise as well as lectures. They were allowed to read newspapers and found it reassuring to learn that the outside world was expressing outrage at their arrest. They sang protest songs and danced Zulu dances. Although they came from different backgrounds they had become united in their common cause. The time spent together gave them a feeling of empowerment. "What distance, other occupations, lack of funds, and police interference had made difficult—frequent meeting—the government had now insisted on," recalled Luthuli.

Two weeks after their arrest the prisoners were summoned to the courthouse. They learned that they were indicted for high treason and conspiracy to use violence to overthrow the government and create a Communist state. The magistrate planned to hold a hearing to determine if there was sufficient evidence to try the case in the Supreme Court. Some of the best lawyers in the country, including Bram Fischer, Vernon Berrange, and George Bizos (who as a boy had left Greece in a boat with his father to escape the Nazis) would represent the accused.

During the hearing the defendants were confined to an area enclosed by wire mesh—much like a cage. Their lawyers could not communicate with them because they were not allowed to enter the cage. The defense protested and, three days later, the court removed the cage. On the fourth day, the judge agreed to release the accused on bail. Several supporters, including Alan Paton and Mary Benson, both white anti-apartheid activists and writers, started a fund to provide bail. The defendants were released but were not allowed to attend public gatherings. They would have to report once a week to the police.

When Mandela arrived home that evening, he discovered his wife and children were gone. He later learned that Evelyn had taken the children to her brother's home. Mandela and Evelyn had developed different interests and their marriage had been fraught with tension; still Mandela had not expected to return to an empty house. While he had been immersed in political activities, Evelyn had become deeply religious, joining the Church of the Jehovah's Witnesses. She wanted Mandela and the children to share her faith,

Crowds cheer as a police van brings prisoners to the Drill Hall, in Johannesburg, on December 31, 1956, for the start of the "Treason Trial." One man has climbed onto the step of the van to shout encouragement to the inmates.

but Mandela had always resisted—he had little time for religion. Other issues also drove them apart. In divorce papers, Evelyn said she left him because of womanizing, neglect, and violence.

As the months wore on, Nelson and Evelyn's separation took its toll on the children. Thembi lost all interest in his studies. Makaziwe ignored her father. Makgatho tried—unsuccessfully— to bring his parents back together.

The Trial for High Treason resumed on January 9, 1957. Defense attorney Vernon Berrange argued that the Freedom Charter was neither treasonable nor criminal. The state produced 12,000 documents—from newspaper clippings to letters and transcripts of speeches—in an attempt to show that the accused wanted to establish a Soviet-style state. Professor Andrew Murray, head of the political science department at the University of Cape Town, testified that the Freedom Charter was communistic; Berrange, however, showed that passages Professor Murray considered problematic were almost identical to statements made by U.S. presidents Abraham Lincoln and Woodrow Wilson, as well as Dr. D. F. Malan, former prime minister of South Africa.

Joe Slovo, representing himself, performed brilliantly in cross-examination and made a good case for the defense by showing that much of the evidence the prosecution presented had been fabricated. By the end of the year the government announced that it would drop the charges against sixty-one of the accused—including Oliver Tambo and Chief Luthuli. However, the magistrate ruled that there was sufficient reason to try the remaining ninety-five defendants. He gave no explanation for why some were chosen and others not.

If the court was not in session, Mandela and the other defendants who had been released on bail were allowed to return to work. One day, when Mandela was at his office, he met a young woman who had scheduled a meeting to discuss a legal matter with Oliver Tambo. The twenty-two-year-old Nomzamo Winifred Madikizela caught Mandela's eye. It was not long before she captured his heart.

Winnie (as she was called) worked as a social worker at a hospital in Johannesburg. She had been born in the Transkei, the daughter of a school headmaster and the great-granddaughter of a chieftain. Winnie's mother had died when she was nine—her father raised her with the help of her two grandmothers. As a child Winnie was a serious student; later, at the age of seventeen, she moved to Johannesburg to study pediatric social work. She would soon become the first black social worker at Bragwanath Hospital.

Winnie and Mandela saw each other frequently, took long walks together, and went for drives. Mandela would often say that he had known he wanted to marry Winnie from the first day he met her. It did not take long for him to ask her to have a wedding dress fitted—Winnie teased him that he had never officially proposed. They were married on June 14, 1958, and Mandela's bans were lifted for six days to accommodate the celebration. The wedding took place at a church in Mbongweni, and a festive reception followed at the home of Winnie's eldest brother. Everyone joined in the singing, and Winnie's grandmother performed a special dance.

Nelson and Winnie in 1958

After her marriage, Winnie joined the ANC's Women's League. Politics appealed to her, and she was soon devoting considerable effort to the freedom struggle. She was tempted to march against the government's ruling that women carry passes—called "reference books." (Failure to do so could result in a ten-pound fine or one-month imprisonment.) But Winnie worried that participation in the march would result in her losing her job at the hospital. She was also pregnant and could be sent to jail. Despite the risks Winnie joined the protest and marched through downtown Johannesburg alongside hundreds of women.

As expected, the police arrested the protesters and put them in jail. On first hearing what had happened, Mandela wanted to arrange bail. But the Women's League president discouraged him: a jail sentence for Winnie and the others would draw much needed attention to their cause. Mandela conceded. The protesters spent two weeks in jail before Mandela arranged bail.

In August 1958, the Trial for High Treason resumed. The state moved the proceedings from Johannesburg to a courtroom—a converted synagogue—in the city of Pretoria. The ANC was less established in Pretoria—the trial therefore would attract less attention. The inconvenience to the defendants was not inconsequential; their long daily commute gave them less time to work or be with their families.

The defense, headed by Afrikaner and Communist Party member Bram Fischer, contested the indictment. To be considered guilty of high treason, the defendants must have planned to use violence. Mandela's attitude towards the use of violence was evolving and, although he had once opposed it, he had become more open to its use. The state, however, could produce no evidence that the ANC had used force.

Several months later the government withdrew its indictment and issued another more precisely worded charge. The indictment against sixty-two of the accused was dismissed. Thirty, however, would stand trial, and Mandela was one of that group.

On February 4, 1959, Winnie gave birth to a baby girl. She was named Zenani, meaning "What have you brought to the world?" Mandela considered the name a challenge to contribute something to the world. "It is a name one does not simply possess but has to live up to."

During this period, the Promotion of Bantu Self Government Act created eight separate Bantustans—or homelands for blacks. Seventy percent of the country's population would be confined to thirteen percent of the land. Many Africans revolted against the Bantu authorities. They were arrested, beaten, and tortured—the press knew little and reported even less. Kaiser Matanzima (Mandela's nephew and Fort Hare classmate) and Winnie's father both supported the Bantu authorities—a distressing situation for Winnie and Mandela, who did not like to find themselves on the opposite side of those they loved. "You probably will not believe it," Mandela confided in a letter to a friend about Matanzima, "when I tell you he was once my idol."

When the trial resumed on August 3, 1959, Mandela and the other twenty-nine defendants pleaded not guilty. The state called 210 witnesses, many of them detectives who had spied on ANC members while hiding in closets or under beds. They played a recording of a speech by ANC leader Robert Resha in which he tells volunteers not to use violence unless they are ordered to do so, adding if "you are called upon to be violent, you must be absolutely violent, you must murder!" The defense argued that Resha was not instructing ANC members to be violent—just to follow orders. The speech was taken out of context, they said, and did not reflect ANC policy.

Chief Luthuli was called as a witness for the defense. Although the prosecution was intent on making Luthuli admit to ties between the ANC and communism, as well as secret plans to use violence, Luthuli calmly and firmly stated his beliefs.

Mandela noted Luthuli's "dignity and sincerity" as he stressed the importance of nonviolent weapons—moral persuasion and economic pressure, such as a boycott of South African goods.

Meanwhile, throughout the country, tension mounted and anger increased. The Pan Africanist Congress, a political group that unlike the ANC did not count whites, Indians, or Communists among its members, planned an anti-pass campaign for March 21, 1960. That morning Robert Sobukwe, the founder of the Pan Africanist Congress, a former ANC Youth League member, and an alumnus of Fort Hare University College, did not carry a pass and turned himself in at the police station. He was sentenced to three years imprisonment.

In Sharpeville, thirty-five miles south of Johannesburg, several thousand Africans—all unarmed—demonstrated against the pass laws. The police, armed with submachine guns and rifles, panicked and started shooting. More than seven hundred shots were fired—four hundred people were wounded and sixty-nine killed. One eyewitness said, "People fell like ninepins." Another reported, "One little boy had on an old blanket coat, which he held up behind his head, thinking, perhaps, that it might save him from the bullets. Some of the children, hardly as tall as the grass, were leaping like rabbits. Some were shot, too. Still the shooting went on. One of the policemen . . . was firing his gun into the crowd. He was swinging it around in a wide arc from his hip as though he were panning a movie camera. Two other officers were with him, and it looked as if they were firing pistols."

The South African Air Force sent out their planes to circle over Sharpeville. "Policemen said later the scene looked like a World War battlefield, with bodies sprawled all around . . . In front of the police station scores of dead and wounded Africans lay sprawled. Blood seeped into the muddy sidewalk and into the gutters," one journalist wrote.

Tom Petrus, an eyewitness to the shooting, later wrote a book entitled *My Life Struggle*, in which he detailed what he saw: "The aeroplanes were flying high and low. The people were throwing their hats to the aeroplanes. They thought the aeroplanes were playing with them. They didn't realise that death was near. . . . People were running in all directions . . . some couldn't believe that people had been shot, they thought they had heard fire crackers. Only when they saw the blood and dead people, did they see that the police meant business."

In Langa, a nonwhite township outside Cape Town, the scene of another protest, six people were killed and two schools destroyed by fire. As news of the bloodshed spread around the world, the UN Security Council denounced the South African government. Assistant Secretary of the ANC Duma Nokwe, Joe Slovo, Walter Sisulu, and Mandela planned a mass protest. They asked Chief Luthuli to burn his own pass and call for a national day of mourning. Luthuli agreed and, on March 26, Luthuli, Mandela, and Nokwe burned their passes publicly. The government declared a state of emergency and instituted martial law.

In the middle of the night on March 30, 1960, the police arrested Mandela—without a warrant. Mandela was taken to a police station in Sophiatown and assigned to a cell with thirty-nine others. The "toilet" consisted of one hole in the ground. No food or blankets were provided. Mandela was chosen to be the spokesperson, and by the end of the following day he had negotiated sleeping mats and blankets. These were "encrusted with dried blood and vomit, ridden with lice, vermin, and cockroaches, and reeked with a stench that actually competed with the odiousness of the drain."

Mandela was sent back to Pretoria and placed in jail. The state of emergency made it difficult for the defense attorneys to meet with their clients; on April 26, the accused announced that they would conduct their own defense. At first the prison authorities tried to prevent the defendants from talking to each other, but they eventually relented, allowing the accused to prepare their own defense.

On August 3, 1960, more than three years after the Trial for High Treason had begun, Mandela was asked to give his own testimony. He stated that he thought democracy could be brought about through gradual reforms. The ANC, he said, was committed to achieving certain demands, including the universal right to vote—without violence.

Chief Luthuli burned his pass in Pretoria on March 26, 1960, and then urged all African people to do the same.

Mandela's words carried great weight. On August 31, the state of emergency was lifted—and the prisoners were released for the duration of the trial. The proceedings would continue for nine months, but Mandela could remain at home.

Mandela and Winnie's five-month separation came to an end. "After one has been in prison," Mandela recalled, "it is the small things that one appreciates, being able to take a walk whenever one wants, going into a shop and buying a newspaper, speaking or choosing to remain silent. The simple act of being able to control one's person."

Mandela in 1960

That December Winnie gave birth to a second daughter, named Zindziswa after the daughter of the Xhosa poet, Samuel Mqhayi, who had given a memorable speech to the students at Healdtown.

By March 1961, the defense was ready to present its final argument. Attorney Issy Maisels spoke clearly: "We shall say quite frankly that if non-cooperation and passive resistance constitute high treason, then we are guilty. But these are plainly not encompassed in the law of treason."

Mandela discussed strategy with the ANC and agreed to continue working for them if the verdict came back "not guilty." He would plan to go underground and live incognito. Winnie realized that regardless of the verdict she would not see her husband: If judged guilty, he would be sent to prison. If innocent, he would go into hiding. The following morning, once again, Mandela said goodbye to his family not knowing when they would be reunited.

On March 29, 1961, the three judges announced their verdict: The prosecution had failed to prove that the ANC had adopted a policy of violence. The accused were to be set free.

Mandela rejoiced as the crowd sang *"Nkosi Sikelel' iAfrika."* "In the case of the Treason Trial," Mandela later wrote, "the three judges rose above their prejudices, their education, and their background. There is a streak of goodness in men that can be buried or hidden and then emerge unexpectedly." Yet across South Africa, racial prejudice remained deeply rooted.

"An Outlaw in My Own Land"

Nelson lived in hiding, sometimes with friends—or, on occasion, in an empty apartment made available by an ANC supporter. Eager to appear inconspicuous and to attract little attention, he grew a beard and dressed as a chef or chauffeur. "I became a creature of the night," Mandela recalled. He slept by day—working mostly in the dark.

Mandela met secretly with newspaper editors, ministers, ANC executives, factory workers, and farmers—often traveling to Cape Town, the legislative capital in the south, and to the province of Natal on the east coast of South Africa. The police were informed about some of Mandela's activities and put out a warrant for his arrest. They set up roadblocks—but to no avail. Mandela could easily elude them. The press started to call him "the Black Pimpernel" after the Scarlet Pimpernel, a character created by novelist and playwright Baroness Emmuska Orczy. The fictional Scarlet Pimpernel—like Mandela—took part in brave exploits, always in disguise.

Not all police were determined to capture Mandela. Those who sympathized with the ANC may have recognized him, but they did not arrest him. Turning a blind eye, they allowed him to attend meetings and travel from one area to another.

Shortly after the Trial for High Treason ended, Mandela helped organize a nationwide "stay-at-home"—or strike—to take place on May 29, 1961. The government prepared for the strike by posting armed guards at power stations, deploying police vans to patrol townships, and recruiting white civilians to serve as constables. Government officials declared that workers who went on strike would lose their jobs.

In an effort to increase support for the anti-apartheid protest, Mandela issued a statement asking "millions of friends outside South Africa to intensify the boycott and isolation of the government of this country, diplomatically, economically, and in every other way." He made the mission of the ANC clear: "Non-collaboration is the weapon we must use to bring down the government. We have decided to use it fully and without reservation."

On the appointed day hundreds of thousands of Africans did not report to work. Participation in Johannesburg was strong— more than half the city's workers stayed home. Throughout the rest of the country the turnout was considerable, but not as high as Mandela had hoped. Although the press called the strike a success, Mandela was disappointed.

Mandela advised the ANC to end the strike. He was again losing faith in nonviolent tactics. The state refused to negotiate or compromise; instead government authorities became more militant—declaring a state of emergency or shooting randomly as they had at Sharpeville. Mandela's goals were ambitious, and he believed that violence might be necessary to win the freedom struggle.

Other ANC leaders remained committed to nonviolence and were extremely reluctant to consider an alternative. Members of the Communist Party advised staying the course; they were not prepared to abandon nonviolence.

Mandela grew exceedingly frustrated. To his colleagues he quoted an African proverb, "The attacks of the wild beast cannot be averted with only bare hands." Mandela was pragmatic. He had formed a simple conclusion: nonviolence would not be effective if the South African government authorities continued to use violent means to quell the protests and enforce apartheid.

Chief Luthuli was still a firm proponent of maintaining a peaceful struggle. Mandela met with the chief and the other members of the executive committee—secretly and at night—to try to win them over. He built a strong case, reasoning that many ANC members, acting individually, had already resorted to violence. They could become far more effective if their efforts became centralized. Mandela argued long into the night.

Educated by American missionaries, Chief Luthuli was a devout Christian. In 1948, he toured the United States, lecturing on Christian missions and advocating the nonviolent practices of both Jesus and Gandhi to oppose the racist policies of the National Party.

Eventually Luthuli and the other ANC executives agreed to let Mandela start a military branch that would remain separate from the main body of the ANC. Members of the Indian Congress voiced their opposition—they wanted no part of a military wing associated with the ANC, even if it were to act independently. They held fast to Gandhi's principles and remained opposed to the use of violence.

J. N. Singh, Mandela's close friend, declared, "Nonviolence has not failed us. We have failed nonviolence." He believed strongly that if they persevered—if they did not lose faith in nonviolence—freedom would be theirs. But again Mandela was tenacious and proved persuasive. His personality prevailed. The larger ANC body allowed Mandela to create a separate military organization.

Having chosen a military course, Mandela now faced new challenges. He was prepared to take risks. His leadership instincts were good—he did not lack for courage. He had a winning disposition as well as determination; what he needed was military training—of which he had none.

Joe Slovo and Walter Sisulu worked with Mandela to organize the new military branch, naming it *Umkhonto we Sizwe* (The Spear of the Nation), "MK" for short. Their manifesto read in part: "The time comes in the life of any nation when there remain only two choices: submit or fight. That time has now come to South Africa. We shall not submit and we have no choice but to hit back . . . [T]he people's non-violent policies have been taken as a green light for government violence. . . . We are striking out along a new road for the liberation of the people of this country."

Mandela, the MK chair, voraciously absorbed new information. He studied military tactics, maps, and the country's transportation system; he read books by Mao Zedong, Che Guevera, and Fidel Castro, the revolutionary leaders of China and Cuba. He analyzed armed struggles in other African countries—guerrilla warfare in Kenya, Algeria, and Cameroon, as well as the struggle against Italian dictator Benito Mussolini in Ethiopia.

In a letter to the people published in South African newspapers on Freedom Day, June 26, 1961, Mandela called for a national constitutional convention. He asked that people fight the government and join him in a battle of noncooperation. He also wrote of the sacrifice he was making—separating himself from Winnie and the children, living "as an outlaw in my own land." He explained, "The struggle is my life. I will continue fighting for freedom until the end of my days."

Mandela kept on the go—moving from place to place when he thought his safety was in jeopardy. In one location his fondness for *amasi*, a traditional Xhosa and Zulu drink that tastes like cottage cheese or yogurt, got him into trouble. While staying with a friend in a white neighborhood, he followed his usual practice of making *amasi*, leaving fresh milk on a windowsill to ferment. Overhearing two black men surprised to see *amasi* on the windowsill, Mandela knew he had aroused their suspicions—he would have to find a new hiding place. Mandela moved to a doctor's house and later to the Liliesleaf Farm in Rivonia, a suburb of Johannesburg, where he posed as a caretaker and called himself David Motsamayi. Other MK recruits soon joined him in Rivonia.

Together the MK leaders worked on their constitution. They debated various tactics—sabotage, guerrilla warfare, terrorism, and open revolution. Mandela did not want to sanction loss of life. He supported restricting violent activity to property damage. Sabotage would become the preferred modus operandi.

In December 1961, Chief Luthuli, the ANC president, was awarded the Nobel Peace Prize for his commitment to racial equality in South Africa. He was praised for his "firm and unswerving approach." In the award ceremony, Gunnar Jahn, chairman of the Nobel Committee, spoke of Luthuli's strong devotion to the freedom struggle. He referred to the difficulties Luthuli faced in a country under apartheid—with restrictive laws and curfews, where there was little security and no decent employment. He also talked of the sacrifices Luthuli had made when he was arrested, banned, and deprived of freedom of movement.

Jahn quoted an excerpt from a letter Luthuli had written to the South African prime minister, Johannes G. Strijdom:

> We believe in a community where the white and the nonwhite in South Africa can live in harmony and work for our common fatherland, sharing equally the good things of life which our country can give us in abundance. We believe in the brotherhood of peoples and in respect for the value of the individual. My congress has never given expression to hatred for any race in South Africa.

The Nobel Prize Committee chair concluded by saying that if nonwhite South Africans achieved freedom "without violence and terror," it would be because of the work of Luthuli. But, if "bloody slaughter" ensues, "Luthuli's voice will be heard no more. . . . He would not have had it so."

The emergence of MK was made public on December 16, 1961, when the group exploded bombs at power stations and government offices in Johannesburg, Port Elizabeth, and Durban—a few days after Chief Luthuli was awarded the Nobel Peace Prize. The irony of the situation was not lost on members of the ANC.

Meanwhile, an international organization, the Pan-African Freedom Movement for East, Central, and Southern Africa, was working to support the liberation and independence of various African countries. The ANC was invited to attend the Pan-African conference in Addis Ababa in February 1962. Mandela was chosen to lead the ANC delegation. He planned to attend the conference and also seek military support for MK from other African nations.

Mandela traveled from Johannesburg to Mbeya and Dar es Salaam in Tanganyika (now Tanzania). He also visited Khartoum in Sudan, Lagos in Nigeria, and Accra in Ghana before arriving in Addis Ababa, the capital of Ethiopia, a country ruled by the legendary emperor Haile Selassie.

Umkhonto we Sizwe targeted Bantu Administration offices, post offices, and other government buildings, as well as railway and electrical installation equipment like the tower pictured here. The first acts of sabotage occurred on December 15 and 16, 1961, and during the next eighteen months two hundred such attacks were carried out. *Umkhonto* members tried to avoid actions that would endanger human lives. Instead, they hoped the acts "would bring the government and its supporters to their senses before it is too late, so that the government and its policies can be changed before matters reach the desperate stage of civil war."

On the first day of the conference Mandela delivered a speech on the history of the South African freedom struggle. He recounted the massacre at Sharpeville and explained that the ANC had failed to achieve its goals through nonviolence. Therefore, he and several others had felt they had no choice but to form a military unit, *Umkhonto we Sizwe* (MK).

After the conference Mandela continued his African tour—stopping in Morocco, Algeria, Mali, Guinea, Sierra Leone, Liberia, and Senegal. Everywhere he went he sought support for his cause. He received advice, as well as weapons training. Mandela also traveled to London, where he met with friends and discussed plans and tactics. Mary Benson, the anti-apartheid activist, took him on a tour of Westminster Abbey and the Houses of Parliament. Mandela later wrote, "While I gloried in the beauty of these buildings, I was ambivalent about what they represented."

Returning to Addis, Mandela started a course in military training. He became familiar with military tactics but was also taught how to treat his cohorts. His mentor and adviser, Colonel Tadesse Biru, explained that he was the leader of a liberation army, not a conventional capitalist army, and he must learn the difference. Mandela must exercise authority "with assurance and control," just as he would with a capitalist army. But as the leader of a liberation army, he needed to treat his soldiers as his equals when they were not on duty. "You must eat what they eat; you must not take your food in your office," he explained.

Mandela had planned to train for six months; after eight weeks, however, the ANC called him back to South Africa. Conditions between the government and the ANC were deteriorating—Mandela would need to take charge.

On his way home Mandela stopped in Dar es Salaam to meet his new recruits. He reminded the men of their mission: "Military training must go hand in hand with political training, for a revolution is not just a question of pulling a trigger; its purpose is to create a fair and just society."

Mandela then flew by private plane to Kanye, a town in southern Botswana. He needed to enter South Africa incognito—if he were recognized he would be arrested immediately. The ANC made arrangements for him to be disguised as a chauffeur. He would cross the border in a car with Cecil Williams, a white theater director and member of MK.

The ruse worked. Mandela returned to South Africa—and yet the police had no clue of his whereabouts.

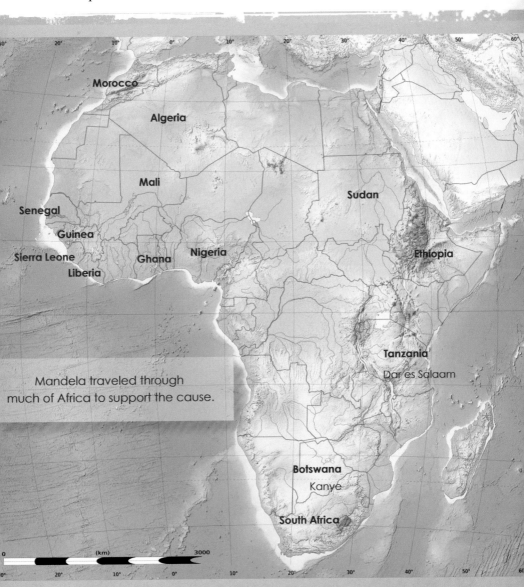

Mandela traveled through much of Africa to support the cause.

SIX

"The Struggle Is My Life"

Back from his travels Mandela returned to the Liliesleaf Farm in the Rivonia suburb. He briefed Walter Sisulu and other ANC leaders on his trip and then quickly departed for secret meetings in Durban. Once again, he was accompanied by Cecil Williams and disguised as his chauffeur. Mandela met with Chief Luthuli to relay messages from foreign leaders, many of whom wanted the ANC to rethink their cooperation with whites and Indians. Chief Luthuli, who had always supported open participation by different racial groups, was disappointed to hear Mandela's report.

While driving back to Johannesburg on August 5, 1962, Williams and Mandela were stopped by the police. Mandela gave the police sergeant the name of his alias—David Motsamayi. The sergeant refused to believe him. Both Mandela and Williams were arrested.

Mandela spent the night in a prison cell—uneasy about the future, wondering who had betrayed him. The next day the police handcuffed him, took him to Johannesburg, and brought him to court. Mandela was charged with inciting African workers to strike and with leaving the country without valid travel documents. Winnie left the courtroom with a heavy heart—her husband could receive as much as a ten-year sentence. Outside hundreds of supporters had gathered. As Mandela passed by them, they shouted, *"Amandla! Nagawethu!"* ("The power is ours!")

African women demonstrate on August 16, 1962, demanding the release of Mandela.

Mandela was imprisoned in the Fort in Johannesburg, and Winnie was allowed only a brief visit. During that time Mandela tried to reassure her. He told her their friends would look after her and reminded her that they both needed to remain strong. She should explain to the children that he might be away for a long time.

A few days later, Mandela was transferred to a prison in Pretoria. Regulations were strict—he was allowed visitors only twice a week. Winnie came to see him whenever she could, bringing clean clothes and much-welcome food. But Mandela spent most days alone in his cell—with plenty of time to prepare his case. He also received permission to take correspondence classes to study for his law degree.

Several ANC members plotted possible escapes and passed on their ideas to Mandela. One plan involved bribes, copies of keys, and a false beard. Mandela rejected the idea, considering it far too risky. He was well aware of how closely he was watched.

The ANC planned a large demonstration in Johannesburg for October 15, 1962, the day Mandela's hearing was scheduled to begin. When the court magistrate caught wind of the preparations for the protest he moved the hearing from Johannesburg to the "Old Synagogue" in Pretoria. Joe Slovo, Mandela's legal adviser, was not allowed to attend since his bans confined him to Johannesburg.

On the day of the hearing, Nelson made a dramatic entrance into the courtroom dressed in traditional Xhosa dress—tribal-length robes and a leopard skin *kaross* (or cloak). His supporters shouted *"Amandla!"* and raised clenched fists. (Later the prison warders would try to confiscate Nelson's *kaross*, but Mandela refused to surrender it.)

During the hearing Mandela explained that he saw no reason to obey laws made by a parliament in which he had no representation. "Why is it that in this courtroom I am facing a white magistrate, confronted by a white prosecutor, escorted by white orderlies?" he asked. "Why is it that no African in the history of this country has ever had the honor of being tried by his own kind, by his own flesh and blood . . . ? I am a black man in a white man's court. This should not be," he continued.

Winnie Mandela wears a traditional dress as she and
two other women attend her husband's trial in Pretoria
on October 22, 1962.

The prosecutor, P. J. Bosch, called more than one hundred witnesses to show that Mandela had incited workers to strike and that he had left the country illegally. He made a good case; there was little to dispute. "The gloves are off now, and it's a fight to the finish against the leftists in South Africa," Bosch declared. He warned that the police would get tougher and that those responsible for sabotage would be punished. "We will get them, and when we do, the full force of the law will be used against them," he added.

Yet secretly Bosch was not happy. Mandela had earned his respect, and he had no desire to send him to prison. Bosch would have much preferred not to hear Mandela's case.

In his final statement Mandela talked about the South Africa he had known as a young boy. Years ago he had moved freely from one part of the country to another. He had listened to the stories the elders told. "Then our people lived peacefully. . . . Then the country was ours, in our own name and right. We occupied the land, the forests, the rivers; we extracted the mineral wealth beneath the soil and all the riches of this beautiful country."

Mandela spoke of joining the ANC, an organization that sought the unity of all Africans and the acquisition of political power for Africans. Over time the white man's government had taken away their rights and imposed laws that proved intolerable. Referring to the government, Mandela declared, "Our consciences dictate that we must protest against it, that we must oppose it, and that we must attempt to alter it." He added, "I was made, by the law, a criminal, not because of what I had done, but because of what I stood for, because of what I thought, because of my conscience."

Mandela explained that the government had provoked violence by using violence to meet nonviolent demands. He did not regret the decisions he had made. He was prepared to pay the penalty, although he had no doubt that posterity would prove him innocent.

After listening to Mandela's speech, the magistrate imposed a harsh sentence—three years for inciting workers to strike and an additional two years for leaving the country without travel documents. Mandela turned away from the magistrate and faced the spectator gallery. He made a clenched fist and shouted *"Amandla!"* The public were prohibited from demonstrating in the courtroom, but once outside they sang *"Nkosi Sikelel' iAfrika"* as they marched through the streets.

Now that Mandela was convicted, his *kaross* could be confiscated. He was issued the prison uniform—a khaki shirt and short trousers. Mandela bristled at wearing short trousers, and he refused to eat the standard prison fare—cold porridge. He was quick to make his complaints known. Eventually he received both long trousers and better food, but he had to pay a price. He would have to accept solitary confinement in exchange for these perks.

Nelson lived apart from the other prisoners in a cell with no window. He was allowed neither books, nor pen, nor paper. He longed for human contact. The isolation proved too difficult, and after several weeks he conceded. He agreed to wear short trousers and eat cold porridge. In exchange, he was moved to a corridor with other political prisoners.

Outside the prison, the military organization known as MK was engaged in acts of sabotage—destruction of property that involved bombings and arson. On May 1, 1963, the government responded by passing the Ninety Day Detention Law. The new law waived the right of habeas corpus so that those suspected of political crimes could be detained without a warrant. Penalties for joining illegal organizations were made more severe—sentences ranged from five years to the death penalty.

Later that month Mandela was one of four prisoners who were told to pack their belongings. They were chained and put in the back of a van with no windows. After driving all night and into the next day, they arrived at the dock in Cape Town, where they were placed inside the hold of a ferry. The boat trip took them eight miles away to Robben Island, which for centuries had been home to a well-known prison.

Mandela and the others were assigned to a cell and fed cold porridge. Mandela felt they were treated like animals. The manual labor they were required to perform, covering up newly laid pipe, was physically demanding. However, one of the warders befriended Mandela and made life more bearable. He often brought Mandela sandwiches—a welcome change from the standard fare.

The prison on Robben Island

After only a few weeks, the prison supervisor informed Mandela that he needed to return to Pretoria. No explanation was given. Mandela later heard that the security police had raided the Liliesleaf Farm in Rivonia. Hundreds of documents were seized— including maps showing power stations, railways, and the homes of policemen. Walter Sisulu, Ahmed Kathrada, Arthur Goldreich, and several other MK leaders were arrested. Mandela would be charged with the others captured at the Liliesleaf Farm.

A few days passed before Mandela and the other prisoners were allowed to meet with their attorneys, Bram Fischer and Vernon Berrange. Fischer broke the news to the defendants: The state was going to try them for sabotage—the prosecution would ask for the death sentence.

Mandela's future looked grim. That night a prison warder told him, "Mandela, you don't have to worry about sleep. You are going to sleep for a long, long time."

On October 9, 1963, the prisoners were taken to the courtroom to hear the indictment. Winnie was under banning orders and not allowed to attend. Walter Sisulu's wife, Albertina, had been detained and also could not be present.

Percy Yutar, the prosecutor, announced that Mandela and ten others were charged with complicity in more than two hundred acts of sabotage and conspiracy to overthrow the government. Defense attorney Bram Fischer stated that the prosecution had spent three months preparing their case whereas the defendants were only just learning the details of their indictment. The judge, Quartus de Wet, was swayed and granted an adjournment.

Mandela and the other prisoners objected that they had been required to wear their prison uniform to court. Mandela especially would have much preferred to dress properly.

The trial resumed three weeks later, on October 29, 1963. This time Mandela was dressed in a suit. The defense argued that the prosecution's case included several inaccuracies. Mandela, for one, had been accused of acts of sabotage at a time when he was being held prisoner in the Pretoria. The prosecution was forced to withdraw their indictment.

The proceedings resumed in early December 1963, after the prosecution had prepared new charges. They called 173 witnesses and alleged that the MK was responsible for 193 acts of sabotage.

However, only a small number of these proved to be linked to the MK. Their most damning evidence was a six-page plan called Operation Mayibuye, a document drafted by Govan Mbeki and Joe Slovo that included a reference to the use of guerrilla warfare.

The defense explained that the document had not been approved by the ANC—Chief Luthuli was unaware of it. Mandela also had not been present when the plan was conceived. He considered Operation Mayibuye impractical and had not favored the use of guerrilla warfare at the time.

The prosecution finished presenting its case on February 20, 1964. Mandela and five of the defendants agreed that they would not deny they were responsible for sabotage. They would explain that they had not engaged in guerrilla warfare, although they might have resorted to guerrilla warfare were sabotage to have failed. They had not committed murder, nor harmed innocent bystanders, nor contemplated the intervention of foreign military forces.

Mandela chose not to provide testimony or submit to cross-examination, but to prepare a statement that would explain his beliefs. The statement would not bear as much weight as testimony; yet Mandela felt he could be more persuasive if he were allowed to speak without interruption.

Mandela rehearsed his statement in front of his co-defendants and Bram Fischer, his attorney. Fischer was alarmed at Mandela's blunt and forceful remarks. He begged Mandela to reconsider. But Mandela refused to make any changes. "I felt we were likely to hang no matter what we said, so we might as well say what we truly believed."

On April 20, 1964, Mandela addressed the court. He denied that the freedom struggle was under the influence of the Communists or foreigners. He admitted to acts of sabotage after "many years of tyranny, exploitation, and oppression of my people by the whites." He spoke of the formation of the MK and stated that their members had been prepared to use force in order to defend themselves against force. Although they had not always succeeded, the ANC and MK had tried to remain separate.

Mandela described South Africa under apartheid: "The lack of human dignity experienced by Africans is the direct result of the policy of white supremacy. White supremacy implies black inferiority. Legislation designed to preserve white supremacy entrenches this notion. . . . Poverty and the breakdown of family life have secondary effects. Children wander about the streets of the townships because they have no schools to go to, or no money to enable them to go to school."

The ANC was fighting to correct these abuses, Mandela explained. "Africans want a just share in the whole of South Africa; they want security and a stake in society. Above all, we want equal political rights. . . . It is a struggle for the right to live."

Life under apartheid saw such scenes as South African police beating African women with clubs in Durban in 1959, after the women raided and set fire to a beer hall in protest against the action of police opposed to their home brewing activities.

Mandela spoke for four hours without notes, and he ended with these words:

> During my lifetime I have dedicated myself to this struggle of the African people. I have fought against white domination, and I have fought against black domination. I have cherished the ideal of a democratic and free society in which all persons live together in harmony and with equal opportunities. It is an ideal which I hope to live for and to achieve. But if needs be, it is an ideal for which I am prepared to die.

Newspapers around the world covered the trial. Vigils were held at St. Paul's Cathedral in London. International trade unions protested. Adlai Stevenson, U.S. ambassador to the United Nations, wrote a letter in support of the defendants. On June 9, 1964, the UN Security Council passed Council Resolution 190 calling for the unconditional release of political prisoners and those who had opposed apartheid.

Two days later, on June 11, Judge de Wet announced the verdict: Mandela was found guilty on four counts of sabotage. Walter Sisulu, Govan Mbeki, Dennis Goldberg, Raymond Mhlaba, Elias Motsoaledi, and Andrew Mlangeni were also found guilty on four counts, including recruiting and training men for guerrilla warfare, preparing for a foreign invasion, and violating the Suppression of Communism Act. Ahmed Kathrada was found guilty on one count.

Mandela, Sisulu, and Mbeki, a former newspaper editor who, like Mandela, had attended Healdtown and Fort Hare, made the decision not to appeal no matter what sentence they received. "I was prepared to die secure in the knowledge that my death would be an inspiration to the cause for which I was giving my life," Mandela said.

The following day both Winnie and Mandela's mother were present in the courtroom. Before the sentence was announced, Alan Paton, author and president of the Liberal Party, spoke on behalf of the accused. Paton did not want to condone violence, yet he recognized that the accused had limited choices—"to bow their heads and submit, or to resist by force." He asked for clemency.

Judge de Wet rose. He appeared under strain, nervous, and uncomfortable. Mandela expected to be handed the death penalty. "People who organize a revolution usually take over the government and personal ambition cannot be excluded as a motive," the judge expounded. The accused had conspired against the government but they had not been tried for, nor found guilty of, treason. Therefore, he could not impose the supreme penalty. The accused—the Rivonia trialists—would receive life imprisonment.

Smiling, Mandela faced the crowd of spectators. He tried to make out the faces of Winnie and his mother, but could not find them.

Winnie (left) is pictured with Mandela's mother, Fanny Nosekeni, outside of the Palace of Justice after hearing that Mandela had been sentenced to life imprisonment.

Alan Paton

"There is a lovely road which runs from Ixopo into the hills. These hills are grass-covered and rolling, and they are lovely beyond any singing of it."

These are the opening words to Alan Paton's *Cry, the Beloved Country*, a novel that gave much of the world its first exposure to the horrors of racial injustice in South Africa. Published in 1948 in New York City, it tells the story of a rural Zulu parson who travels to Johannesburg in search of his missing sister and son, Absalom, whom he discovers is a suspect in the murder of a white man. The priest loses his faith and ultimately regains it. By the time of Paton's death in 1988, *Cry, the Beloved Country* had sold more than 15 million copies in twenty languages.

seven

On Robben Island

"Well, you chaps won't be in prison long. The demand for your release is too strong. In a year or two, you will get out and you will return as national heroes," one of the police officers said to Mandela and the other Rivonia trialists. They were in a van on their way to a military airport where they would board a plane that would take them to Robben Island. Mandela felt encouraged—he would not die in jail; before long he would be a free man once more.

The Robben Island prison, where the men were incarcerated, was a secure stone fortress. Armed guards—and large German Shepherd dogs—patrolled the catwalk of a twenty-foot wall. The accommodations were rudimentary at best. Each prisoner was assigned a small cell with a window one-foot square. When Mandela lay down to sleep on his sisal mat his head touched one wall of the cell and his feet the other.

Police join hands to hold back demonstrators outside the court in Pretoria on June 12, 1964, after eight of the accused in the Rivonia Sabotage trial, including Nelson Mandela and Walter Sisulu, were sentenced to life imprisonment.

The Rivonia trialists were awakened every morning at 5:45 a.m. The black prisoners were issued short trousers. However, Ahmed Kathrada, an Indian, was allowed long trousers. There were no toilets; they had to use iron buckets instead. For breakfast they were given mealie pap porridge (cereal made from corn) and a drink that was called coffee but was really ground corn and water. Every morning they were made to work in enforced silence—crushing stones into gravel. They ate soup for lunch and afterwards returned to their work.

When they finished at 4 p.m. they were allowed to wash in cold seawater in a bathroom. They took supper in their cells—more mealie pap porridge, occasionally carrots, cabbage, or beetroot, and every other day a small piece of meat. Indian and Coloured prisoners received bread and butter, but blacks did not. In the evenings talking was discouraged—the warders wanted to prevent any communication.

The warden divided the prisoners into four classifications—A, B, C, and D—and granted privileges accordingly. All political prisoners started with a "D"—the lowest category. The "D" prisoners were allowed one visitor every six months; they could write and receive only one letter during that time. Whatever mail prisoners received was censored. Prison guards would black out parts or use razor blades to cut out offending passages. Winnie's first letter to Nelson was filled with so many black marks that few legible words remained.

By the end of August 1964 Winnie succeeded in arranging a visit to Robben Island. She had to agree not to speak Xhosa or mention anyone besides her children or "first-degree" relatives. When the couple met they were not allowed to be in the same room but had to communicate through thick glass that had a few holes drilled through it. Mandela assured Winnie that he was in good health, and Winnie relayed news about the family. The thirty-minute visit was all too fleeting.

Permission for visits was rarely granted. Winnie would not be allowed to return for two years.

In January 1965, the Rivonia trialists were assigned to work in a lime quarry. They were given picks and shovels and told to extract the lime from the layers of rock—it was backbreaking work. The authorities never gave any explanation for the change in routine. Mandela assumed they wanted to remind the Rivonia trialists that they would not receive special treatment.

The men had to labor for long stretches of time. The dust was thick and the heat intense. Still, Mandela found it invigorating to be out in the open. He also enjoyed the opportunity to converse with his fellow prisoners—silence was not enforced at the quarry. They discussed a wide range of topics, from the relationship between the ANC and the Communist Party to the presence of tigers in Africa.

The prison warden told the men it would take them six months to complete their task. Little did they know they were to spend thirteen years at the quarry.

In the evenings the Rivonia trialists were allowed to study— a privilege Mandela and others very much appreciated. Kathrada was well aware that much depended on his "mental attitude;" he tried to make the most of his studies, adopt a "broad outlook," and "leave little time for pettiness and idle thought." His self-taught course work was extensive—history, anthropology, economics, and the Xhosa language.

Mandela studied law by taking correspondence classes with the University of London. Not everything went smoothly—book delivery could be inexplicably denied. At first none of the cells were equipped with desks so Mandela could only study sitting on his sisal mat. When representatives from the International Red Cross visited, Mandela complained about the situation. Before long the prison authorities were installing primitive stand-up desks in the cells.

Many of the prisoners formed study groups and enjoyed learning from each other. Walter Sisulu offered a course in the history of the ANC. In a political economy course Mandela compared and contrasted feudalism, capitalism, and socialism. Mandela also prepared legal appeals for other prisoners; in some cases their verdicts were overturned or their sentences reduced.

Prison gave Mandela time to reflect and reminisce. In a letter to his sister he wrote of missing their homeland, his school, and the river where they had bathed. Thinking about the freedom

Mandela's cell was very small and sparse.

struggle, he contemplated the future of the movement, the role he had played, and the character traits of a strong leader. In a letter to Winnie, he wrote:

> We tend to concentrate on external factors such as one's social position, influence and popularity, wealth and standard of education . . . but internal factors may be even more crucial in assessing one's development as a human being: honesty, sincerity, simplicity, humility, purity, generosity, absence of vanity, readiness to serve your fellow men—qualities within the reach of every soul.

The Rivonia trialists craved information about the outside world, but the prison authorities enforced a news blackout. Prisoners bribed warders for a copy of a newspaper or they surreptitiously retrieved the newspaper in which the warders' lunch sandwiches were wrapped. Reading a newspaper was not without risk. When Mandela was caught with a paper his punishment was severe: he had to spend three days in isolation and was not allowed to eat.

In July 1966, Winnie visited Robben Island for the second time. In the brief period allotted to her she expressed her concern about the education of their two daughters. Zenani and Zindziswa were attending an Indian school but were made to feel unwelcome. Mandela agreed with Winnie to send them to a boarding school in the nearby country of Swaziland.

Winnie's daily life was filled with constant challenges. When she returned from Robben Island she was expected to check in with the police. But she neglected to do so. She was arrested and tried—receiving a one-year sentence. Winnie spent four nights in jail before her sentence was suspended. She was released but soon lost her job as a consequence of the negative publicity surrounding the Rivonia trial. The government banned Winnie, thereby prohibiting her from visiting her children's schools. Winnie would deeply regret never meeting her daughters' teachers.

The prisoners on Robben Island found it difficult to keep track of time. One day seemed much like any other. In a letter to friends Kathrada wrote that "the years roll by very quickly in jail—it's the minutes and hours that go rather slowly." For Mandela time stood still; he was frustrated knowing "it did not halt for those outside." The police officer who had predicted that the Rivonia trialists would be released within a few years was sadly mistaken. There was no telling if or when they would become free.

As the months and years passed Mandela savored the memory of each visit and visitor. In 1967, Nelson received a visit from Helen Suzman, the only member of Parliament who belonged to the Progressive Party. She was concerned about the welfare of the political prisoners—and had come to investigate. Mandela made a good first impression. She noted his "imposing stature" and "his easy way of communicating." The other prisoners looked to him as their leader. Mandela reported to her on the food, clothing, study facilities, availability of newspapers, and the attitude of the warders—he had a long list of complaints. As a result, the most offensive warder, who had charged the prisoners with insubordination at the slightest provocation and urinated next to them while they ate lunch at the quarry, was dismissed.

Helen Suzman

But seven years would pass before Helen Suzman was again granted permission to visit Robben Island.

In the spring of 1968 Mandela's mother, his son Makgatho, his daughter Makaziwe, and his sister Mabel paid a brief visit to Robben Island. Mandela was shocked to see the changes in his family. His mother's health was deteriorating—she had grown thin and very old. His children had now become adults. Mandela had trouble accepting that he had played such a small role in their adolescence.

A few months later Makgatho sent a telegram to say that Mandela's mother had died of a heart attack in September. Mandela wanted very much to attend her funeral, but he was denied permission. He was distressed to have to miss the funeral—and also sad to think that under different circumstances he might have been able to make his mother's life more comfortable. "I had never dreamt that I would never be able to bury ma," Mandela wrote in a letter to Winnie's stepmother. "On the contrary, I had entertained the hope that I would have the privilege of looking after her in her old age, and be on her side when the fatal hour struck."

It was a difficult period for Mandela. He learned that Winnie had again been detained. This time she was placed in solitary confinement in Pretoria. She was denied bail and charged under the Suppression of Communism Act—to be released seventeen months after her arrest.

Mandela wrote to his daughters to share his concerns. He told them that their mother must be "twenty-four hours of the day longing for her little ones." He worried that they would "live like orphans" and he commiserated, "Now you will get no birthday or Christmas parties, no presents or new dresses."

In one letter to Winnie, he wrote, "I feel as if I have been soaked in gall, every part of me, my flesh, bloodstream, bone and soul, so bitter am I to be completely powerless to help you." In other letters he urged Winnie to remain strong. He also reminded her of their courtship days.

Their correspondence became his lifeline. Mandela could be charming, flirtatious, serious, or morose. In answer to one of Winnie's letters he wrote, "If there was ever a letter which I desperately wished to keep, read quietly over and over again in the privacy of my cell, it was that one. It was compensation for the precious things your arrest deprived me of—the Xmas, wedding anniversary, birthday cards—the little things about which you never fail to think. But I was told to read it on the spot and [it] was grabbed away."

In July 1969 Nelson received a second telegram from Makgatho. It read: "Please advise Nelson Mandela his Thembekile passed away 13th instant result motor accident in Cape Town." Mandela read the telegram, lay on his bed, and would not talk. Later Walter Sisulu visited him in his cell to keep him company, but still Mandela did not speak. He grieved for his son, who had died at the age of twenty-four. He wrote that the death "left a hole in my heart that can never be filled."

Mandela asked for permission to attend his son's funeral, but it was denied. He wrote Evelyn a letter expressing his sorrow. In a letter to Winnie he recalled the last time he had seen his son. During the Rivonia case Thembi had sat behind him in the courtroom. Mandela would turn to look at him, but his son never smiled. "At the time it was generally believed that we would certainly be given the extreme penalty and this was clearly written across his face. . . . I never dreamt that I would never see him again. That was five years ago."

As time wore on Mandela noticed that conditions on Robben Island were improving. Prisoners were issued long trousers and uniforms that fit. They could talk freely and were permitted to play cards and games such as chess, checkers, Scrabble, and bridge. They were allowed to attend church services. African prisoners received bread at meals, a staple that had previously only been offered to Indians and Coloureds. And on Christmas the Rivonia trialists would purchase sweets and organize a concert—a medley of English, African, and protest songs.

Over the years the Rivonia trialists had developed friendships with several of the warders. Kathrada noticed that their relationships became not only "cordial," but "decidedly warm" with "considerable exchange of small talk." One warder was on such good terms with Mandela that he hatched an escape plan. The warder was to furnish Mandela with a key to the prison, a boat, and underwater diving gear. Mandela thought the plan too far-fetched and did not follow up. (He later discovered the warder was acting as an agent for the Bureau of State Security.)

This was not the only time Mandela considered running away. One of the prisoners with whom he had become friendly urged him to make an appointment with a dentist sympathetic to their cause. Mandela planned to visit the dentist in Cape Town and then slip away from his guards. He followed through with the appointment, but once he arrived, he suspected something was not right. Looking out the window, he saw that what was normally a very busy street was empty. Fearing he had been set up, he had his teeth cleaned and returned to prison.

Another plot involved arranging for a helicopter to take Mandela to the roof of the Zambian embassy where he could then seek asylum. The risk of failure was too great. Mandela stayed put.

With Mandela and his fellow Rivonia trialists locked up, and the rebellion of the early 1960s suppressed, South Africa and its controlling white minority prospered. The economy's rate of growth over the period 1960-70 averaged nearly 6 percent a year, second only to Japan's. An American writer commented, "At some point around 1970 white South Africans overtook Californians as the single most affluent group in the world." In stark contrast, most Africans in South Africa lived in poverty.

In the early 1970s, the South African government renewed its efforts to establish independent homelands, or territories, for blacks; one of them was the Transkei where Mandela was born. Jimmy Kruger, the minister of prisons, presented Mandela with an offer: He would reduce Mandela's sentence if Mandela agreed to accept the new policy and move to the Transkei. Mandela refused. He would not support the policy nor would he agree to live in the Transkei. Johannesburg was his home.

Zindzi, Mandela and Winnie's daughter, paid a visit to her father in 1975, shortly after she turned fifteen. (Winnie had changed her birth certificate so that it would appear that she was sixteen, the minimum age for visitation rights.) Mandela—who had not seen his daughter since she was three—was thrilled, struck also by how much she resembled her mother. Zindzi too was pleased to meet her father and found him a "very diplomatic, charming man." She was relieved to see he still looked "fit and strong."

On July 18, 1975, Mandela's fifty-seventh birthday, Walter Sisulu and Ahmed Kathrada urged their good friend to write his memoirs—with the thought that they would be published in time to celebrate his sixtieth birthday. Mandela liked the idea and immediately set to work on the project. Several prisoners helped in the process. Sisulu and Kathrada wrote comments and suggestions in the margins of the manuscript. Laloo Chiba, formerly a tailor and a member of MK, copied the manuscript in miniscule handwriting. They planned for their friend Mac Maharaj to smuggle the copy out of prison upon his release at the end of the year.

Mandela wrote long into the night. Within four months he had completed the manuscript. He did not want to destroy the original until he was assured that Maharaj had safely delivered the transcribed version to a publisher. Mandela divided the original manuscript into three parts, wrapped each one in plastic, and buried them in the courtyard garden. But, a few weeks later, he saw a work crew digging in the garden—in the same place where two portions of the manuscript were buried. He told Sisulu and Kathrada. They waited for the crew to take a break and then quickly uncovered the two parcels. They left the third untouched. Since it was hidden under a pipe the prisoners thought the workmen would leave it alone.

The men were sadly mistaken. The third parcel was discovered and brought to the attention of the warden. He recognized Mandela's handwriting, as well as Sisulu and Kathrada's notes in the margins, and issued a severe penalty—the suspension of study privileges for four years. It was a devastating blow.

However, Maharaj was released in December 1975 and took with him the transcribed version—bringing it safely to London. It was not published at the time and was presumed lost—only to resurface in 1994.

On June 16, 1976, 15,000 schoolchildren took to the streets in Soweto to protest the use of Afrikaans—the language of the oppressor—in school. In the riot that followed, a thirteen-year-old boy, Hector Pieterson, was killed, and hundreds of children were wounded. Two white men were stoned to death. In the next few days more riots broke out across the country. Teachers resigned and parents joined the protest. In sixteen months between six hundred and one thousand were killed (two were white, the others black), and almost 4,000 were wounded.

Many of the young rioters were sent to Robben Island. The Rivonia trialists were eager for news and heartened to learn that the struggle was gaining momentum. Mandela was buoyed by their rebellious spirit. He was also stunned to witness the brashness of their behavior. Many did not think twice about disobeying prison regulations. Mandela came to see that he would no longer be considered one of the most radical prisoners on Robben Island.

Mandela later learned that Winnie had also been detained and imprisoned after the student riots. Upon her release her anger turned to fury, and she became increasingly more militant. The police sent Winnie and her daughter Zindzi to Brandfort township in the Free State, two hundred and fifty miles southwest of Johannesburg, where they were forced to live simply with no heat or running water. Winnie did not stay idle—she was allowed to start a childcare center and raise funds for a clinic. However, in the evening and on weekends, she was placed under house arrest and could not be in the company of more than one person at a time.

By 1978, the Rivonia trialists had started to balk at the manual labor they were expected to perform at the quarry. They spent more time chatting than working. It became clear that little was accomplished. Finally, the supervisors stopped trying to enforce manual labor and allowed the prisoners to take up other activities.

Mandela gardened, played tennis, studied, and read. Although many books were banned, he had a wide range of choices. He enjoyed reading Tolstoy's *War and Peace*, John Steinbeck's *The Grapes of Wrath*, and novels by Daphne du Maurier. Old movies— westerns or black and white Hollywood films—were shown once a week. Mandela took particular pleasure in this new "privilege": "The films were a wonderful diversion, a vivid escape from the bleakness of prison life," he wrote.

Meanwhile, Mandela's daughter Zenani had fallen in love with Thumbumuzi Dlamini, a prince from Swaziland. Soon after marrying in 1978 they started a family. As members of the Swazi royal family, they received diplomatic privileges and could visit Mandela in prison. Zenani and Thumbumuzi brought with them their baby daughter. It was a special moment for Mandela. "To hold a newborn baby, so vulnerable and soft in my rough hands, hands that for too long had held only picks and shovels, was a profound joy," he wrote. "I don't think a man was ever happier to hold a baby than I was that day." He was asked to name the child and he called her Zaziwe—meaning *hope*.

eight

"Time to Talk"

In the late 1970s, partly in response to international pressure, the South African government tried to make life on Robben Island a little more pleasant. The warden offered a greater variety of films—documentaries and South African films with black stars. Prison officials started their own radio news service in 1978. The news was biased and censored, but it did provide the prisoners a small window onto the world.

In 1980 two newspapers became available—the *Cape Times* and *Die Burger*. However, both publications were censored—the Rivonia trialists did not see the papers until various articles had been removed with scissors.

That same year, Mandela received the Jawaharlal Nehru Award for International Understanding, an annual award previously given to Mother Teresa and Martin Luther King Jr. Mandela wrote an acceptance speech and arranged for it to be smuggled out of prison and sent to Oliver Tambo, then living in exile in London. Tambo traveled to Delhi to accept the award on behalf of his good friend.

In his speech Mandela paid tribute to Gandhi, who had shown that "no people in one part of the world could really be free while their brothers in other parts were still under foreign rule." Mandela underscored Nehru's belief that nationalism "blinds us to many happenings and sometimes distorts the truth, especially when it concerns us and our country." He ended with Nehru's visionary message: "'If the future we work for is full of hope for humanity, then the ills of the present do not matter much and we have justification for working for that future.'"

In March 1982, Mandela was told to pack his things. Walter Sisulu and two other Rivonia trialists, Raymond Mhlaba and Andrew Mlangeni, received the same instructions. They were not instructed where they were going, only that they were being transferred.

Mandela had spent eighteen years on the island and was sorry he was not allowed to say good-bye to friends and staff. "A man can get used to anything," he wrote, "and I had grown used to Robben Island."

A ferry took the four men to Cape Town, and from there they were driven a few miles southeast to Pollsmoor Prison. They were assigned to the top floor—one spacious room with four beds (and sheets) and a separate bathroom (with towels). They shared an L-shaped terrace—also very large. Once he settled in, Mandela enjoyed being outside and took up gardening—cultivating a wide variety of vegetables that were used to feed the prisoners and even the warders.

Mandela and the others received no explanation for the move and speculated that the government had wanted to isolate leaders of the freedom struggle so they could not influence others on the island. Their suspicion was confirmed when Ahmed Kathrada, another political leader, later joined them at Pollsmoor.

Years in prison had helped the men cement their bond. In a letter to his niece, Kathrada wrote that the men had become his extended family—Walter ("a gentle, caring person") was like an uncle to him, and Mandela an older brother. They had come to know each other well—they had told the same jokes many times and if one were to start a story, the other could easily finish it.

When Winnie visited her husband, both she and Mandela found that the supervision was more humane. They were still separated by glass, but they could see each other from the waist up, the microphones worked well, and the officer in charge was polite. Starting in May 1984, Mandela was allowed "contact visits"—he could now be in the same room with Winnie. Mandela recalled, "It had been twenty-one years since I had even touched my wife's hand."

News reached the prisoners at Pollsmoor more easily and swiftly than it had on Robben Island. In August 1982, Mandela learned that anti-apartheid activist Ruth First—Joe Slovo's wife— was killed by a car bomb. This came as a blow to Mandela—he was fond of Ruth and had admired her for a long time. They had first met in 1943 when they were both students at the University of Witwatersrand.

Mandela, left, talks to Ruth First, center, outside the court during the first treason trial in 1957.

Ruth First's death did little to instill fear in the freedom fighters or to silence their movement. Around the world the cause gained momentum. In 1984 Bishop Desmond Tutu, an anti-apartheid supporter, received the Nobel Peace Prize. In his presentation speech, Egil Aarvik, chairman of the Norwegian Nobel Committee, praised Desmond Tutu: "[A]lthough he has never learnt to hate, none has opposed injustice with a more burning anger." He had sought "the peaceful way to freedom" and used weapons of spirit, reason, and indignation.

In his Nobel Lecture, Desmond Tutu described the inhumane conditions of squatter camps in South Africa and spoke of the "unacceptable price" people had to pay for apartheid. "There is no peace because there is no justice," he explained. He concluded with a call for action: "Let us beat our swords into ploughshares."

Desmond Tutu

Print media and television news reported on the consequences of South African apartheid, the brutality of the police, and the struggle and courage of blacks, Coloureds, and Indians. Anti-apartheid activists were pushing economic sanctions—efforts on the part of foreign governments to ban trade with South Africa. The efficacy of sanctions was debated in living rooms, around kitchen tables, and in editorial columns across the United States, as well as on the Senate floor. Senator Edward Kennedy campaigned relentlessly for the U.S. to divest—or relinquish assets—from South Africa, to impose sanctions, and to end all financial support of the apartheid regime.

Throughout his 1984 campaign for the presidency Reverend Jesse Jackson brought attention to injustice in South Africa. In his electrifying address at the Democratic National Convention on July 18, 1984, he decried apartheid, calling a partnership with South Africa "a moral disgrace."

In late 1984, Mandela was allowed to meet with two respected public figures—Lord Nicholas Bethell from the British House of Lords and Professor Samuel Dash from Georgetown University in Washington, D.C. Mandela discussed prison conditions but also the liberation movement and his personal vision for the future: a state without homelands; nonracial elections for parliament (as opposed to quotas for different groups); and a one-person, one-vote system.

On January 31, 1985, P. W. Botha, the South African president, publicly offered Mandela his freedom—were he to unconditionally reject violence. Mandela refused. He favored a solution that would involve negotiation, not war, but he would not accept Botha's condition. Mandela was not convinced that the state would also reject violence, nor make the necessary reforms to establish a just and democratic government.

Mandela prepared a public response to Botha's offer. On February 10, 1985, Mandela's daughter Zindzi read his statement at the Jabulani Stadium in Soweto. Mandela had written that he was

Zindzi Mandela reads the refusal of her father, Nelson, to leave prison on February 10, 1985, in Johannesburg, after South African president P.W. Botha offered him conditional release.

not a violent man, but that it was "when all other forms of resistance were no longer open to us, that we turned to armed struggle." He called on President Botha to renounce violence, un-ban the ANC, and free those who were imprisoned for their opposition to apartheid. And he asked, "What freedom am I being offered while the organization of the people remains banned? . . . What freedom am I being offered when I must ask for permission to live in an urban area? What freedom am I being offered when I need a stamp in my pass to seek work? What freedom am I being offered when my very South African citizenship is not respected?"

Later that year Mandela required prostate surgery and was treated in a hospital in Cape Town. When he returned to the Pollsmoor Prison he was given his own suite of rooms on the ground floor. No explanation was given for the change; he later suspected that he was being groomed to take on a more important role in planning a new form of government.

Living alone gave Mandela more time to think. He concluded that loss of life was not inevitable—he could achieve his goal without resorting to violence. He needed to remain open to the possibility of negotiation. "It was time to talk," he said, and he would proceed without discussing his decision with Walter Sisulu, Ahmed Kathrada, Ray Mhlaba, or Andrew Mlangeni. Mandela did not want to give them the opportunity to dissuade him.

In February 1986, leaders from nations of the British Commonwealth had met to discuss international sanctions against South Africa. They had decided to appoint a group of "Eminent Persons" to conduct a fact-finding mission in South Africa. General Olusegun Obasanjo, former military leader of Nigeria and a member of this group, planned for the delegation to meet with Mandela. When the government learned about the meeting, they arranged for a fitting with a tailor so that Mandela would have a proper suit for the occasion.

Meeting with the "Eminent Persons" delegation, Mandela discussed the need for greater communication between the government and the ANC. The solution was to be found through negotiation—both parties would need to renounce the use of force. The "Eminent Persons" delegation planned to relay Mandela's thoughts to the South African Cabinet ministers. However, on the day of the scheduled meeting, the South African Defense Force launched air raids on ANC bases in Zambia, Zimbabwe, and Botswana. The meeting was canceled.

On June 12, 1986, the government announced a state of emergency. The police surrounded townships, blocked roads, and detained thousands of black people. Mandela asked to meet with

Kobie Coetsee, the minister of justice. Coetsee agreed, and an amicable meeting followed. The two men discussed the suspension of the armed struggle and changes in government. Mandela requested a meeting with the president and foreign minister.

Months passed without further developments. The deputy commander of the prison took Mandela for a drive through Cape Town and bought him a soft drink—Mandela's first city excursion in twenty-two years. On other occasions warders accompanied Mandela to the beach or took him to a café. Mandela never learned why he was given special treatment, but he wondered if the government thought he would be more likely to make concessions if he had experienced moments of freedom.

Finally, in 1987, Coetsee informed Mandela that a committee of senior officials would like to meet with him. This time Mandela thought he should first consult with the other ANC leaders at Pollsmoor. Kathrada was opposed to negotiation and Sisulu slightly reluctant, but both men said they would not stand in his way. Raymond Mhlaba and Andrew Mlangeni favored negotiation.

When Oliver Tambo learned of the possibility of negotiations he wrote to Mandela to express his reservations. Mandela tried to reassure him: His goal was only to set up a meeting between the ANC National Executive Committee and the South African government; he would not compromise on his principles.

Meanwhile, members of the Afrikaner intelligentsia and the ANC's exiled leadership were holding secret meetings in a stately manor outside of London. These talks had been initiated by Consolidated Goldfields, a British mining company with deep financial interests in South Africa's future. By the late 1980s, many leading Afrikaners, particularly members of the Broederbond, the secret Afrikaner society with close ties to the government, wanted to find a way to end the government policies of racial separation. But they also wanted to maintain control of the country as well as secure protection of their cultural heritage. The twelve talks started in late 1987 and would continue over several years, with ANC exile Thabo Mbeki, son of Govan Mbeki, acting as the ANC's lead negotiator.

Back in South Africa, meetings with Mandela started in May 1988 and continued throughout the year, often weekly, sometimes less frequently. The government committee wanted the ANC to renounce violence. Mandela answered that if the oppressor used violence, the oppressed would respond violently. The committee also questioned the ANC's relationship with the Communist Party. Mandela explained that they were two separate organizations, yet they both supported a nonracial South Africa.

Public support to free Mandela was already strong. The film *Cry Freedom*, directed by Richard Attenborough, had helped raise the consciousness of people in the U.S. and Europe. The film tells the story of Steve Biko, an activist in the anti-apartheid movement who took the lead in the Soweto student uprisings. This Black Consciousness Movement leader was arrested in August 1977 and died less than a month later. The police blamed his death on a hunger strike, but wounds on his head showed signs of torture and brutal beating.

Mourners surround the coffin of Steve Biko on September 25, 1977, in his home. A mirror on the raised lid of the coffin reflects the gold-robed body.

The popularity of a new musical called *Sarafina* also added to international pressure to release Mandela. Written by Zulu composer and playwright Mbongeni Ngema, *Sarafina* opened in New York in October 1987 and soon created a Broadway sensation—drawing attention to the student riots in Soweto, police brutality, and the spirit and resilience of a young schoolgirl named Sarafina while raising the public's awareness of the evils of apartheid. *Sarafina*'s freedom songs became international hits. The cast—twenty-three South African performers and seven band members—toured throughout the U.S., Europe, Australia, and Japan.

During the summer of 1988 celebrations of Mandela's seventieth birthday were held in various cities around the world. A rock concert in London featured Harry Belafonte, Whitney Houston, and Roberta Flack. Stevie Wonder performed "I Just Called to Say I Love You"—a song he had dedicated to Mandela.

At Pollsmoor Prison, Sisulu and Kathrada were allowed to meet with Mandela to wish him a happy birthday. Kathrada noticed that Mandela could barely talk and worried about his cough. Mandela was soon admitted to a hospital where he was treated for tuberculosis, the illness that may have taken the life of his father. He spent several months in a comfortable clinic and eventually recuperated.

On December 9, 1988, Mandela was moved to the Victor Verster facility in Paarl, northeast of Cape Town. He was taken not to the prison but to a cottage behind it. His new house had a living room, a large bedroom, two small bedrooms, and a swimming pool. There were guards—but no bars.

The following day, Kobie Coetsee visited him and explained that he had arranged the move so that Mandela could be in an environment where he could comfortably host meetings. Discussions with the committee continued. Helen Suzman from the Progressive Party was allowed to visit. A meeting with President Botha was planned, but the president suffered a stroke in January 1989 and the meeting was canceled. For months no one mentioned a date for a meeting between Botha and Mandela.

Finally, on July 4, 1989, Mandela received word that he would meet with the president the following day. Mandela was driven to Tuynhuys—the Cape Town office of the president. President Botha smiled when he met Mandela, putting him immediately at ease. The two men shook hands and posed for photographs. They were served tea and discussed history and culture. Mandela waited until the end of the meeting to ask the president to release all political prisoners—including himself—unconditionally. Botha firmly but politely rejected his request.

There would be no follow-up with Botha. In August 1989, the president resigned and F. W. de Klerk, the minister of national education and the new head of the National Party, became acting president. Mandela did not know what to expect. He was to discover that de Klerk saw change "as necessary and inevitable."

On October 10, 1989, de Klerk announced that Sisulu, Kathrada, Mhlaba, Mlangeni, and three other Robben Island prisoners would be released. After opening South African beaches to all people, de Klerk planned for the repeal of the Reservation of Separate Amenities Act—the law that segregated parks, theaters, restaurants, buses, libraries, and toilets.

On December 13, 1989, Mandela was again taken to Tuynhuys, this time to meet with President de Klerk. For the first time Mandela felt that a National Party leader was trying to listen and understand his position. Mandela conveyed his concern over the National Party's "group rights" proposal. This plan would ostensibly extend rights to minority groups; in effect it would preserve white domination.

Mandela also stated other concerns. He asked that the ANC become un-banned, the state of emergency lifted, political prisoners released, and exiles allowed to return. President de Klerk answered that he would take Mandela's requests under consideration.

Less than two months later, on February 2, 1990, de Klerk announced a change in policy: Bans on the ANC were lifted and political prisoners freed. "Our world had changed overnight," Mandela wrote.

South African president F. W. de Klerk announces the unconditional release of jailed ANC leader Nelson Mandela, the unbanning of the ANC, PAC, and South African Communist Party, and the lifting of the state of emergency during parliament in Cape Town on Friday, February 2, 1990.

The following week de Klerk again called for a meeting in his office. When Mandela entered, de Klerk was smiling. The two men shook hands, and de Klerk then informed Mandela that he would be released the next day.

Mandela was taken aback. Although he was overjoyed, he had little time to prepare. His release from prison would not only bring happiness to his family and friends, but it also signified an important moment in history. He wanted to make the most of it.

On February 11, 1990, Winnie and Walter Sisulu joined Mandela at the Victor Verster prison, and they shared a special meal to celebrate the occasion. Mandela thanked the officer who had prepared it, not only for the food, but also for the companionship he had provided while Mandela lived at Victor Verster. Mandela bore him no ill will.

Mandela and Winnie left the cottage in a car and stopped a quarter mile outside the entrance to the prison. As they walked toward the gate they were astonished by the number of people—reporters, photographers, old friends, and young admirers, many of them overcome by emotion. Lost in the multitude of people were the warders and their families—Mandela regretted not having the opportunity to say good-bye to them.

Free after twenty-seven years, Mandela turned to face the crowd and raised his right fist. In some ways he had not changed at all—he was still tall and thin and he carried his head high. But in one important way he was entirely different from the willful man who had walked onto Robben Island in 1964. Said Mandela of himself: "I came out mature."

Nelson Mandela and Winnie walk hand in hand with their raised clenched fists upon Mandela's release from Victor Verster prison, near Cape Town.

nine

"Never Again"

"Suffering can of course embitter the one who suffers. But in many other circumstances it can ennoble the sufferer. We were richly blessed that the latter happened with Mandela," Archbishop Desmond Tutu wrote.

Tutu was quick to notice that his old friend had changed. Mandela had grown "in magnanimity and generosity of spirit"—for now he understood "the fears and anxieties of his adversary." It was difficult for those in power to relinquish control, not knowing what the future would hold. Mandela had become less angry. He stood on principle—but he was willing to compromise.

Throughout the long freedom struggle, Tutu had remained close to Mandela and Winnie. He had admired their courage and had asked Winnie to be the godmother to his grandchild. As soon as Mandela was released he welcomed the Mandelas into his home in Bishopscourt, a suburb of Cape Town. Friends and family joined them there, elated that the years in captivity had at last come to an end. Mandela basked in the warmth of the reunion. He missed his good friend Oliver Tambo but later that night enjoyed speaking to him by telephone.

Mandela and Winnie in the garden of Archbishop Desmond Tutu's residence

Mandela and Winnie did not stay long in Cape Town. Archbishop Tutu's wife phoned them to say that the people in Johannesburg longed to see him. Thousands of supporters had surrounded their Orlando home in anticipation. Mandela and Winnie flew by helicopter to Soweto and landed in the center of the stadium. One hundred and twenty thousand people—all ebullient—had gathered to hear him speak and celebrate his freedom.

South Africa had become transformed. The country once dominated by white supremacy had now become open to the possibility of a more inclusive government. Although they had not fully embraced a nonracial society, National Party leaders were willing to listen to the voice of a black man. Before going to prison Mandela, considered by the majority of white South Africans as both a dangerous man and a threat to society, had lived in hiding. Now, twenty-seven years later, he had become popular and much-loved, a force larger than life; he was esteemed, believed to be both powerful and wise.

"Today, my return to Soweto fills my heart with joy," Mandela said. "At the same time I also return with a deep sense of sadness. Sadness to learn you are still suffering under an inhuman system."

The people were poor; problems relating to the housing shortage and unemployment were overwhelming; crime was rampant.

In many places Mandela found the poverty worse than when he went to prison. There was much work to be done. ANC leader and economist Max Sisulu, son of Walter and Albertina Sisulu, commented, "The effect of apartheid on children has been terrible. You've got a whole generation that was unable to go to school. Unemployed people who have just been roaming the streets. . . . You've got children—young kids as little as nine or ten—who have been arrested and jailed."

But Mandela had a way with people. He made them want to help bring about change. He was self-assured; he had a commanding presence but was not authoritarian.

Soon Mandela was traveling throughout Africa to obtain support for a new democratic form of government from leaders of different countries. Enormous crowds greeted him wherever he went—in Dar es Salaam there were a half million well-wishers. Mandela also traveled to Sweden for an emotional reunion with Oliver Tambo, still in exile, and to London for a concert in his honor at Wembley Stadium. The concert was televised to 1 billion viewers around the world. When Mandela appeared on stage during the finale the audience broke into cheers. Mandela thanked all those who had pressed for sanctions and shown solidarity to the cause.

In March Mandela had been scheduled to begin formal talks with President de Klerk. However, negotiations were put on hold after an incident of police brutality in Sebokeng Township, thirty miles south of Johannesburg, not far from Sharpeville where the 1960 massacre had occurred. At an ANC rally on March 26, 1990, the police attacked demonstrators, killing twelve people and wounding 163. Of the thirty policemen who fired into the crowd, eighteen were "instant constables" who had received an average of seven hours of training. They had used penetrating ammunition, instead of the less dangerous "birdshot" they had been instructed to carry.

Although the formal talks were canceled, Mandela did meet privately with de Klerk. Mandela had hoped de Klerk would agree to "majority rule," but he was still favoring "group rights" that would allow the whites to maintain power. Blacks would be allowed to vote and write legislation; still, whites would retain a veto power.

Mandela and a delegation that included Walter Sisulu, Joe Slovo, and Ahmed Kathrada met for three days of formal talks with the government in April. The delegation demanded that elected representatives begin writing a new constitution and that an interim government be established to oversee the transition to the new government. After making some progress the two sides pledged to continue peaceful negotiations.

In June, Mandela returned to Europe, visiting France, Switzerland, Italy, the Netherlands, and England. While Mandela was away, the South African government, as it had promised, lifted the state of emergency.

Mandela flew from London to the United States, where he continued to adhere to a demanding, tightly scheduled itinerary. He went from one event to another with little or no time to rest. He led a fast-paced life—it was as if he was making up for lost time.

In New York, hundreds of thousands turned out to see Mandela when his forty-car motorcade took him through the city. Ticker-tape—in record amounts—fell from skyscrapers. The Empire State building was lit in green, black, and gold—the colors of the ANC flag.

"We have risen up on the wings of angels," he told the 2,000 people who filled Riverside Church on New York's Upper West Side on June 21. "We have walked and not fainted. Our destination is in sight. Our victory will be your victory." Mandela thanked the congregation at the ecumenical service, many of whom were long-time supporters: "During the long years when we were in prison, you did not forget, neither did you abandon our struggling people."

Mandela also asked for support in maintaining sanctions: "To lift sanctions now, before we have seen profound and irreversible

Wall Street area workers wave and throw ticker tape as Mandela's vehicle passes during a parade through lower Manhattan on June 20, 1990, in New York.

change in apartheid, would be a serious political error. It would plunge us back into the darkness from which our country is painfully struggling to emerge."

Civil rights activist Reverend Jesse Jackson was one of a diverse group of religious leaders who spoke: "As dramatically as the Red Sea opened, as dramatically as the walls of Jericho came tumbling down, the walls of Berlin came tumbling down, let the walls of apartheid come tumbling down." African singers and drummers, a gospel choir, and a brass quartet took part. The congregation danced in the aisle and, for a brief moment, Mandela joined them.

Mandela planted a tree in Harlem in memory of the South African schoolchildren who had died in the 1976 riots in Soweto. He used soil from Soweto for the tree planting—a symbol of their shared struggle and the bond between the two.

He spoke at a Harlem rally—100,000 people strong. At Yankee Stadium he attended a concert in his honor with performances by Judy Collins, Richie Havens, and Tracy Chapman. Wherever he went he was given a hero's welcome.

Mandela gave an address to the Special Committee against Apartheid at the United Nations. He flew to Boston to have lunch with Senator Edward M. Kennedy to thank him for his support. He met with President George H. W. Bush in Washington and addressed a Joint Session of Congress. His message was consistent:

Nelson Mandela, deputy president of the African National Congress, acknowledges applause as he stands before a Joint Session of Congress on Capitol Hill in Washington.

He urged his audience not to repeal sanctions, declaring, "To deny any person their human rights is to challenge their very humanity . . . . We have fought for the right to experience peace." He reminded Congress that he and other freedom fighters "went to jail because it was impossible to sit still while the obscenity of the apartheid system was being imposed on our people. It would have been immoral to keep quiet while a racist tyranny sought to reduce an entire people into a status worse than that of the beasts of the forest."

Back in South Africa Mandela discovered that progress was slow, anger more intense, and violence more pervasive. Both blacks and whites thought civil war was imminent. White extremists viewed de Klerk as a traitor. Joe Slovo suggested the ANC agree to stop the armed struggle so that negotiations could proceed. After initially balking, Mandela supported the proposal. He now had to persuade other ANC leaders to lay down their arms. On August 6, 1990, the government and the ANC signed an agreement called the Pretoria Minute—the armed struggle was suspended, and more political prisoners were released.

Mandela had now chosen a different path. He had become a peacemaker, or what Archbishop Desmond Tutu called "an icon of forgiveness and reconciliation." Mandela embraced all religions—preaching tolerance, openness to diversity, and service to humanity. People in South Africa and around the world saw in Mandela what Tutu so much admired, "a passion for integrity and honesty and respect for the inherent dignity of every person."

Mandela believed he owed a debt to Gandhi for inspiring him and members of the ANC Youth League to set in motion the Defiance Campaign. This campaign had been inspired by satyagraha—the nonviolent civil resistance movement Gandhi had first used to win rights for Indians in South Africa. Now, thirty-eight years after the Defiance Campaign, South Africa was poised to become free and democratic. Once again Mandela stood firm in the belief that he could achieve his goal peacefully—through negotiation.

Mandela traveled around the countryside to see first hand the hardships his people faced. In many communities racial tension and rivalries between various political parties had led to bloodshed. Mandela was disheartened to learn of the preponderance of violent acts of rebellion. Antagonism between the ANC and the Inkatha Freedom Party (IFP), an anti-apartheid party led by Mangosuthu Buthelezi, a Zulu chief and a former ANC Youth League member, was rife. The IFP, the vast majority of whom were Zulu, exerted great influence and control in rural areas. A militant branch of the IFP opposed the ANC and wanted to establish a Zulu king as head of state in the province of Natal. Mandela suspected that the police and defense forces helped to destabilize the region by confiscating weapons from the ANC and handing them over to the Inkatha.

In July 1990, Mandela learned that members of the Inkatha Freedom Party were planning an attack on ANC members in the Sebokeng township. ANC attorneys informed the police, yet no action was taken. On July 22, busloads of armed Inkatha members entered the city, accompanied by police. At a rally later that day thirty men were killed. Mandela informed de Klerk of the atrocities and asked why the police had not responded. De Klerk promised to investigate but never gave an explanation.

Mandela and Chief Buthelezi, the head of the Inkatha party, reached an accord to end the violence—but it was never implemented. The fighting continued—the police did nothing. Over three days in March 1991, forty-five people were killed in Alexandra Township, north of Johannesburg. Again the police made no arrests. The ANC believed the police incited much of the bloodshed.

Despite the unrest, plans for the formation of the new government proceeded. The first ANC conference to be held in South Africa in thirty years took place in July 1991. The 2,244 delegates who attended the conference elected Mandela ANC president by a unanimous vote. He was succeeding Oliver Tambo, who had served as president since Chief Luthuli's death in 1967.

On December 20, 1991, the government, the ANC, and other political parties started serious negotiations. Meetings of the Convention for a Democratic South Africa (CODESA) took place at the World Trade Centre near the Johannesburg airport with observers from the UN in attendance. Mandela assured the assembled group that progress was now irreversible and that an elected assembly would soon write a new constitution.

On the first day de Klerk accused the ANC of maintaining a private army and not adhering to the peace agreements. Mandela was stunned and expressed his disappointment with de Klerk's remarks. De Klerk should not have publicly criticized the ANC; after all the National Party had also not acted openly—they had funded covert organizations to undermine the ANC.

Meanwhile, Winnie was experiencing her own personal difficulties. In 1991 she was convicted of kidnapping and becoming an accessory to assault in connection with the death of fourteen-year-old James Seipei (also known as Stompie Moeketsi). Allegedly, Seipei was murdered because he was a suspected police informer. Winnie received a six-year prison sentence, but it was reduced to a fine on appeal. Mandela supported his wife while she faced criminal accusations, just as Winnie

James "Stompie" Seipei

had supported him. They both cared deeply about the formation of the new country, yet their approaches differed drastically and created friction between them. When abused or marginalized, Winnie was quick to show her anger. Mandela felt no bitterness and was ready to move on.

Winnie's troubles didn't end there. In 1992, she was stripped of her office in the ANC's Women League, following charges that she misused ANC funds. The same year Mandela announced his separation from his wife. He expressed his gratitude for the comfort she had provided during the many years he spent in prison. He admired her loyalty to the freedom struggle, and he had no recriminations. But Winnie had long been romantically linked to the lawyer who had represented her in the Seipei case. Mandela had found a letter written to Dali Mpofu by Winnie, in which she declared her love for him. This was the proverbial straw that broke the back of their thirty-eight-year marriage.

Later Mandela spoke of the difficulties freedom fighters experienced. He was sorry not to have spent more time with his wife and family. He had always known there would be challenges and sacrifices, but he had not known how hard they would be. "When your life is the struggle, as mine was, there is little room left for family. That has always been my greatest regret, and the most painful aspect of the choice I made."

The second round of negotiations—CODESA 2—was held in May 1992. Mandela warned de Klerk that the whole world was watching—they had to save the peace process. Still they made little headway, disagreeing on issues that would give whites more power, such as an unelected senate with veto power over the main parliamentary chamber.

During the night of June 17, 1992, about two hundred Zulus armed with knives, pangas, and guns massacred forty-six people, mostly women and children, in a squatter camp in Boipatong, a dusty, obscure township south of Johannesburg. The attackers came from a nearby migrant workers' hostel that was a stronghold of the Inkatha Freedom Party. No arrests were made—and de Klerk remained silent. The ANC suspended the CODESA 2 negotiations, accusing the ruling National Party of complicity in the attacks.

President F. W. de Klerk, right (behind the window), watches protesters while on a visit to Boipatong, on June 20, 1992, to sympathize with victims of the massacre. Angry blacks cursed de Klerk and forced him to abort his visit.

As the bloodshed increased, both Mandela and de Klerk became more determined to see the negotiations succeed. On September 26, 1992, they signed the Record of Understanding: An independent body would review police actions—killings in rural areas would no longer be ignored. The government also agreed to accept a single, elected assembly; a new constitution would be adopted. The tide had turned.

Joe Slovo proposed establishing "a government of national unity," a temporary measure that would give the National Party power for a fixed period of time, grant amnesty for security officers, and honor contracts of civil servants. Mandela supported the proposal but insisted that the minority party not have a veto.

Secret talks with the government at a game lodge followed. The ANC and the government agreed to a plan for a five-year government of national unity—all parties polling more than 5 percent would be proportionately represented in the cabinet. After five years, a majority-rule government would take over.

Hopes for a peaceful transition were jolted on April 10, 1993, when Chris Hani, general secretary of the South African Communist Party and a former leader of MK, was shot outside his home in Johannesburg. The country's youth considered Hani a hero—he had devoted his life to helping the poor and disadvantaged. His efforts to integrate residential neighborhoods and his support for the peace process had led to his assassination.

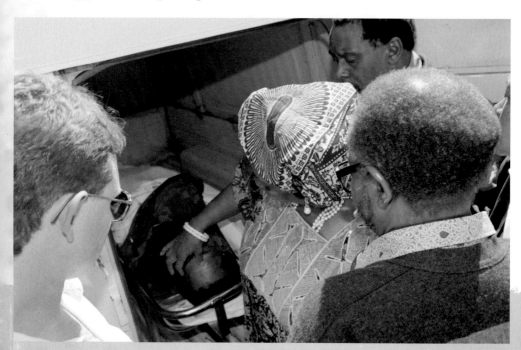

Adelaide Tambo, center, wife of former president of the African National Congress, Oliver Tambo, closes the eyes of assassinated South African Communist Party leader Chris Hani after his body was placed in a van in Boksburg.

The political atmosphere was tense—some thought a racial war might erupt. Mandela spoke to the nation in a televised address. He asked all South Africans to stand together and he encouraged white people to join in memorials for Hani. He said:

> This is a watershed moment for all of us. Our decisions and actions will determine whether we use our pain, our grief, and our outrage to move forward to what is the only lasting solution for our country—an elected government of the people, by the people, and for the people.

He urged the police to act with sensitivity and called on the youth "to act with wisdom."

Two weeks later Mandela faced another loss that touched him deeply. Oliver Tambo, now living in Johannesburg with his wife Adelaide, suffered a stroke. Adelaide phoned Mandela to alert him. Mandela tried to see Tambo one last time, but he arrived too late. He felt "like the loneliest man in the world."

Speaking at Tambo's funeral, Mandela said:

> A mind whose thoughts have opened the doors to our liberty has ceased to function. A heart whose dreams gave hope to the despised has forever lost its beat. The gentle voice whose measured words of reason shook the thrones of tyrants has been silenced. Peoples of the world! Here lies before you the body of a man who is tied to me by an umbilical cord which cannot be broken.

Mandela regretted that Tambo would not live to see South Africa's first free election. On June 3, 1993, the South African government, the ANC, and the other political parties agreed that the first one-person/one-vote election in South Africa would be held in April 1994. People of all races and ethnicities would elect delegates to an assembly that would write a constitution and serve as a parliament. The assembly would also be charged with electing a president. The struggle for which Mandela had devoted his life was won.

The Nobel Prize Committee recognized the significance of Mandela and de Klerk's achievement and awarded them the Nobel Peace Prize in 1993. Mandela and de Klerk traveled to Norway for the ceremony. Mandela spoke as a representative of the millions of people "who dared to rise up against a social system whose very essence is war, violence, racism, oppression, repression and the impoverishment of an entire people." After paying special tribute not only to Chief Albert Luthuli and Archbishop Desmond Tutu, the two South Africans who had previously won the peace prize, but also to Martin Luther King, Jr., he ended with a plea: "Let the efforts of us all prove that he was not a mere dreamer when he spoke of the beauty of genuine brotherhood and peace being more precious than diamonds or silver or gold."

Meanwhile, preparations for the election continued. ANC candidates, introduced to the public at People's Forums, outlined the creation of new jobs, the building of new homes, schools, and clinics, and the redistribution of land. Difficulties arose when the Inkatha Freedom Party (IFP), the Conservative Party (a political party opposed to ending apartheid), and the Afrikaner People's Front (a right-wing organization) voiced their opposition to the coming election and threatened not to participate. They feared the ANC would dominate and that they would lose all political influence. The ANC proposed compromises to guarantee greater powers to people living in rural areas, thereby assuring that these parties would retain some of their power. Chief Buthelezi, head of the Zulu-based IFP, agreed to participate only after a constitutional role for the Zulu monarchy was offered.

A television debate between Mandela and de Klerk took place ten days before the election. Mandela accused the National Party of spreading hatred between races. But, as the debate ended, he

Mandela and de Klerk with their Nobel Peace Prize Gold Medal
and Diploma, in Oslo, December 10, 1993

proved more conciliatory: "I think we are a shining example to the entire world of people drawn from different racial groups who had a common loyalty, a common love, to their common country." He concluded, "We are going to face the problem of this country together."

On April 27, 1994, at the age of seventy-five, Mandela cast his first vote. Five days later, after all the votes were counted, Mandela announced the ANC victory to a crowd assembled at the Carlton Hotel in Johannesburg: "I watched, along with all of you, as the tens of thousands of our people stood patiently in long queues for many hours, some sleeping on the open ground overnight waiting to cast this momentous vote." Mandela shared his pride in the country's achievement: "You have shown such a calm, patient determination to reclaim this country as your own. What joy that we can loudly proclaim from the rooftops—free at last!"

It was a day to remember. The ANC, the party to which Mandela had dedicated most of his life, captured 62.6 percent of the vote. Mandela would become his country's first black president.

On the eve of his inauguration, the future president addressed the people of Cape Town, telling them they had come together to celebrate "not the victory of a party, but a victory for all the people of South Africa." Mandela outlined an ambitious agenda for change that included promoting peace and reconciliation, tackling widespread poverty, creating jobs, encouraging investors, easing credit conditions, increasing manufacturing opportunities, and healing wounds of the past.

On May 10, 1994, Nelson Mandela was sworn in as president, Thabo Mbeki (an ANC leader who had spent twenty-eight years in exile) as first deputy president, and F. W. de Klerk as second deputy president. To the 4,000 foreign dignitaries and South Africans present at the inauguration and to the 1 billion television viewers, Mandela spoke these words:

[W]e, who were outlaws not so long ago, have today been given the rare privilege to be host to the nations of the world on our own soil. . . . We know it well that none of us acting alone can achieve success. . . . Never, never, and never again shall it be that this beautiful land will again experience the oppression of one by another. . . . The sun shall never set on so glorious a human achievement!

Mandela had helped his people on "the long walk to freedom," yet he was well aware they had not reached their destination. "I can rest only for a moment, for with freedom come responsibilities," Mandela reflected.

Members of the Moledi family in Soweto watch a live broadcast of the inauguration of President-elect Nelson Mandela in Pretoria, May 10, 1994. Mandela was sworn in as South Africa's first black president.

ten

"Madiba"

Although a longtime prisoner Mandela quickly grew accustomed to his role as president—adjusting gracefully to a new home, new office, and new life. His training in Mqhekezweni in the house of the regent Jongintaba had prepared him well.

Mandela spent time in the country's two presidential offices, one in Pretoria and the other in Cape Town—and he established homes in both cities. He kept to a strict schedule, waking early at 4:30 a.m., making his own bed, taking a walk before breakfast, punctual to all appointments. Mandela quickly developed a fondness for his staff—both black and Afrikaner. He made them all feel comfortable, and they in turn remained loyal and devoted. They called him "Madiba"—referring with respect to the name of his clan.

After his separation from Winnie, Mandela found a partner to share both his work and his life. On a trip to Mozambique in 1990, Mandela had met Graça Machel, the widow of Samora Machel, the country's former president. He saw her again two years later when she visited Cape Town to receive an honorary degree—and after that he continued to see her as often as possible. Before long Graça was spending two weeks a month in Johannesburg—returning in between to her home in Maputo, the capital of Mozambique.

South African president Nelson Mandela, left, and Graça, wife of the
late Mozambican president Samora Machel, right, during a Sunday
afternoon stroll through a Johannesburg suburb

The former minister of education and culture in Mozambique,
Graça had been a longtime advocate of children's causes. She
researched and wrote a detailed report for the United Nations,
Impact of Armed Conflict on Children. She conducted extensive
interviews—talking to nine-year-old girls who had been raped by
soldiers, as well as to ex-child soldiers abandoned by their families.
Published in 1996, the report provided proposals for the international community to monitor and protect children in war zones.
Graça also provided support to Mandela as he struggled to establish the new form of government—overcoming a wide range of
difficulties, some predictable and others unexpected.

During his five-year term in office Mandela's devotion to a nonracial democracy where all people were treated equally never wavered. Always wary of a possible coup or revolt, he paid close attention to defense and security issues. For advice he often turned to Ahmed Kathrada, now a newly elected member of Parliament. He also relied on his first deputy president, Thabo Mbeki, as well as the cabinet. At meetings he developed the habit of listening to each member before expressing his own views. Decisions were reached by consensus.

In June 1995, South Africa played host to the Rugby World Cup—a welcome reminder that a new democratic era was beginning. (South Africa had not been allowed to take part under the apartheid regime.) Mandela supported the country's first-time participation in the major sporting event—seeing it as an opportunity to bring together a divided country. The South African Springboks were an all-white team with the exception of one Coloured member. Many blacks were uninterested in the game and cared little for the outcome. Rugby was associated with white supremacy and a way of life they wanted to leave behind. Most whites suspected their black president was indifferent to the outcome of the tournament. Mandela surprised them all by taking a keen interest in the game—showing tremendous support for the team and, by example, encouraging the black population to do the same.

South Africa—unexpectedly—advanced to the finals. They played their last match against New Zealand. At halftime they led 9-6. But, at the end of regulation time the two teams were tied. When the Sprinboks made the winning goal in overtime, the cheering was deafening.

Mandela wore a green Springbok jersey as he strode onto the field to present the captain, Francois Pienaar, with the prize trophy. The ecstatic crowd—mostly white—went wild—chanting "Nelson, Nelson." The mood across the country was jubilant and celebratory as citizens of all colors rejoiced. The victory pleased

Mandela—it had helped unify the country. His political instincts had proved correct.

The culture of South Africa was in flux—Mandela's strategy was working. His spirit remained undaunted. His goal was to create not only a non-racist state, but one that was non-sexist. He was eager to give women a voice and assure that they were no longer powerless as they had been under apartheid. The old patriarchal South Africa had allowed millions of black women to remain illiterate. Mandela was determined to change that.

Cyril Ramaphosa, a lawyer and trade union leader who had worked with Mandela to negotiate the new government with the National Party, was heading the parliamentary committee to write the new constitution. After much discussion and many compromises, the committee finished its preparations in October 1996. Parliament quickly ratified the proposed constitution.

Yet, throughout the country, many were slow to embrace the new form of government. Racial disputes continued and tension mounted. Mandela saw little evidence that the nation's wounds had healed. Determined to bring about racial harmony, Mandela launched the Truth and Reconciliation Commission.

This Commission, chaired by Archbishop Tutu, gathered statements from 21,000 victims who had suffered during the freedom struggle. During the four years that followed, government officials, politicians, and security forces confessed to a myriad of crimes and human rights violations, committed to enforce and perpetuate apartheid. The State Security Council admitted to authorizing their forces to "neutralize" opponents—in keeping with President Botha's orders.

Mandela, a strong believer in "the power of the truth to heal," told the public, "We can forgive but we can never forget." He wanted to assure that the past would not repeat itself. On April 27, 1997, he told the crowds gathered in Upington in the Northern Cape to celebrate Freedom Day, saying, "The best recompense that can be made to the victims, and the most powerful substance for reconciliation, is our success in building a new society."

The Truth and Reconciliation Commission prepared a five-volume report that held all sides accountable—the state government as well as the ANC. Amnesty was granted to those who revealed the truth about their misdeeds and crimes. But the publication of the report proved controversial. De Klerk had been accused of concealing knowledge of bombings; when de Klerk objected, the reference was blacked out in the report.

The ANC also tried to suppress information about their execution of twenty-two ANC members for offenses that included mutiny, rape, and murder. References to these crimes were not omitted—Bishop Tutu prevailed in publishing an uncensored accounting.

Other South Africans responded to the report by asking for a general amnesty. Mandela rejected this, favoring only individualized amnesty. He wanted those who did not confess their guilt to recognize that they could be tried at a later date. He believed forgiveness was necessary, but that there had to be an admission of guilt. If no effort were made to investigate the crimes or hold the perpetrators accountable, the ensuing anger would lead to mass revolt.

After receiving the report from the Commission, Mandela thanked the thousands of men and women who had shared their loss and pain, as well as the hundreds who had admitted their guilt. Mandela believed the Commission had laid the foundation of reconciliation, and he wanted his people to be secure in their faith in two words—"Never Again!" He reminded his audience that the "further construction of that house of peace needs my hand. It needs your hand." He stressed the importance of continuing the struggle to end malnutrition, homelessness, and ignorance.

In 1997, at the age of seventy-nine, Mandela relied more on his deputy Mbeki, who proved eager to take on increased responsibility. Mandela decided to step down as ANC president. At the fiftieth conference of the ANC, Mandela thanked the African National Congress for making him who he was, and said, "I look forward to that period when I will be able to wake up with the sun, to walk the hills and valleys of my country village, Qunu, in peace and tranquility."

The following year, on Mandela's eightieth birthday, July 18, 1998, Nelson and Graça were married at their home in Johannesburg. A Methodist bishop, assisted by Archbishop Desmond Tutu, performed the ceremony. The next day, more than 2,000 guests were invited to celebrate the wedding. Mandela's grandson Mandla and Thabo Mbeki, now president of the ANC, gave speeches in honor of the newly wedded couple. To the great delight of the guests, Mandela and his new wife danced what became known as "the Madiba shuffle."

Mandela spent the last year of his presidency working to improve his country, providing his people with access to clean water, electricity, housing subsidies, new roads, free health care, nutrition programs, and jobs for women as well as men. He struggled to fight crime and improve the police and security forces. He found ways to increase investment, productivity, and exports—and to rely more on manufacturing and tourism and less on agriculture and mining. "History will judge us," he said, "by our success or failure in turning the tide of poverty."

Yet, despite Mandela's efforts, crime was escalating. Military equipment and weapons were stolen—the security and armed forces fell under suspicion. Political groups became associated with criminal gangs, and warlords were assassinated. A large number of whites fled the country. The violence and the white flight disturbed Mandela—he started campaigns to establish partnerships between communities and police. While he tried to create more jobs, some of his efforts proved unsuccessful.

"[T]here is no time to pause. The long walk is not yet over. The prize of a better life has yet to be won," Mandela reminded members of Parliament on February 5, 1999.

Before leaving office, Mandela and Graça traveled together to several countries—Argentina, Brazil, Britain, the Netherlands, Scandinavia, and the United States. Throughout the world Mandela had become a well-known advocate of human rights and was greatly admired for his wisdom and persuasiveness.

On March 29, 1999, Mandela gave his last speech to Parliament, saying, "It is in the legislatures that the instruments have been fashioned to create a better life for all." He paid tribute to all South Africans who had made him who he was—the villagers, the workers, the intelligentsia, the business people, and those who "cherished the vision of a better life for all people everywhere." He ended with the words, "The long walk continues."

Outgoing South African president Mandela (left) and incoming president Thabo Mbeki (right) follow a parliamentary staff bearer as they leave Parliament on June 14, 1999, in Cape Town.

Since stepping down as president, Mandela has devoted his time and energy to bringing peace and stability to his country, to supporting the Nelson Mandela Children's Fund (which he started in 1995), to promoting educational reform and a non-segregated school system, to raising awareness about environmental issues, and to campaigning for care and compassion to all those who live with HIV/AIDS. (His youngest son died of AIDS.) "AIDS knows no custom," Mandela says. "It knows no colour. It knows no boundaries."

Mandela also tried to project a much more rounded image of himself, through the release of jailhouse writings and letters and in one-on-one interviews. "One issue that deeply worried me in prison was the false image I unwittingly projected to the outside world; of being regarded as a saint," he told one interviewer. "I never was one, even on the basis of the earthly definition of a saint as a sinner who keeps trying."

On May 5, 2003, Mandela lost his longtime friend, comrade, and mentor. Walter Sisulu died at the age of ninety in the arms of his wife Albertina. Walter and Albertina had devoted their lives to the freedom struggle; their children also became anti-apartheid activists. After Mandela arrived in Johannesburg in 1941, Walter had taken him under his wing—introducing him to the ANC. Ever since their first meeting Walter had remained a loyal friend to Nelson—a brilliant and unassuming mentor. After he died, Mandela explained, "He stood head and shoulders above all of us. What was the reason for this? Because he had the gift of humility and simplicity."

The flag of South Africa

In Qunu, the poor but beautiful hamlet where Mandela spent his boyhood, there is a redbrick bungalow sitting high on a hill, overlooking a dairy and fields growing corn, beans, and pumpkins. The bungalow is Mandela's; it is his belief that "a man should die near where he was born." The residence is modeled on the floor plan of the house in which he was incarcerated at Victor Verster prison until his release in February 1990. Nearby is a second, bigger house, where he celebrates Christmases, birthdays, and other holidays, surrounded by friends and family, many of whom still live in Qunu. One of his grandsons is the chief of nearby Mvezo, the tiny village where Mandela was born.

Qunu is also close to the wandering hills, valleys, and streams that Mandela has so wistfully spoken of throughout the years, and near to the river where he was initiated into manhood as a sixteen-year-old. Then, the young initiate had wondered if he was indeed brave. Today, few will question whether Mandela, an icon of freedom and forgiveness and one of the greatest moral guardians of the modern age, has proven himself brave beyond measure.

Nelson Mandela

Timeline

1918	Born to Gadla Henry Mphakanyiswa and Nosekeni Fanny on July 18 in Mvezo in the Transkei; named Rolihlahla.
1919	Moves to Qunu, after his father is stripped of his chieftainship.
1927	"Adopted" by Jongintaba, the Thembu regent, after his father, Chief Henry, dies of an undiagnosed lung disease.
1934	Sent to Clarkebury Boarding School.
1936	Attends Healdtown, a Methodist mission college.
1939	Attends University College of Fort Hare; meets Oliver Tambo.
1941	Runs away to Johannesburg.
1943	Joins the African National Congress (ANC).
1944	Marries Evelyn Mase; the couple will have four children.
1948	Elected national secretary of the ANC Youth League.
1950	Plans a National Day of Protest on June 26.
1952	Starts the Defiance Campaign, a mass protest against unjust laws; arrested and found guilty.
1953	Banned; writes "No Easy Walk to Freedom" speech.
1955	Helps write the Freedom Charter, the new constitution for the ANC.
1956	Arrested and charged with high treason.
1958	Marries Nomzamo Winifred (Winnie) Madikizela; they will have two daughters, Zenani and Zindziswa.
1961	Found not guilty as the Treason Trial ends; organizes a military unit called MK.
1962	Travels throughout Africa and to London to gain support for the ANC; arrested, convicted, and imprisoned.
1964	Stands trial for sabotage; sentenced to imprisonment for life; transported to Robben Island.
1965	Begins hard labor in lime quarry.
1975	Starts his memoirs.

1978	Zenani, her husband, and daughter visit Mandela in prison.
1982	Moves to Pollsmoor Prison outside Cape Town.
1984	Allowed "contact visits" in prison.
1986	Meets with Kobie Coetsee, minister of justice, to discuss future of South Africa.
1988	Moves to Victor Verster facility in Paarl.
1989·	Meets with President P. W. Botha in July; starts negotiations for a free and democratic government with his successor, President F. W. de Klerk.
1990	Freed after twenty-seven years in prison; travels throughout Europe and the United States to rally support for anti-apartheid movement.
1993	Shares the Nobel Peace Prize with President F. W. de Klerk.
1994	Elected president as the ANC claims victory in the country's first free election.
1995	Plays host to the Rugby World Cup.
1996	Launches the Truth and Reconciliation Commission; divorces Winnie.
1998	Marries Graça Machel on his eightieth birthday, July 18.
1999	Retires as president of South Africa after one term; hands power to Thabo Mbeki.
2001	Diagnosed and treated for prostate cancer.
2004	Retires from public life.
2005	Son, Makgatho, dies of AIDS.
2007	Grandson, Mandla, installed as chief of the Mvezo Traditional Council.
2008	Turns ninety.
2009	Votes for the fourth time in his life.
2011	Celebrates ninety-third birthday with family in Qunu.

Sources

Chapter One: Son of a Village Chief

p. 9,   "At dawn . . ." Nelson Mandela, *Long Walk to Freedom: The Autobiography of Nelson Mandela* (New York: Little, Brown and Company, 1994, 1995), 27.

p. 9,   "Ndiyindoda! . . ." Ibid., 27.

p. 9,   "I felt ashamed . . ." Ibid.

p. 10,   "a tall, dark-skinned man . . ." Ibid., 5.

p. 11,   "My father . . ." Ibid., 6.

p. 12,   "a clever . . ." Ibid., 12.

p. 12,   "a very noble man," Chief Anderson Joyi, "The Long Walk of Nelson Mandela Interviews: Chief Ndaba Mtirara, Chief Anderson Joyi and Chief Jonginyaniso Mtirara," PBS.org, http:www.pbs.org/wgbh/pages/frontline/shows/mandeal/interviews/chiefs.html.

p. 16,   "the brutal clash . . ." Ibid., 41.

p. 16,   "I remember walking . . ." Mac Maharaj and Ahmed Kathrada, eds., *Mandela: The Authorized Portrait* (Kansas City, MO: Andrews McMeel Publishing, 2006), 15.

p. 16-17, "There sit our sons . . ." Ibid., 29-30.

p. 19,   "They (the whites) call . . ." *Reader's Digest Illustrated History of South Africa: The Real Story* (Cape Town: The Reader's Digest Association South Africa Ltd., 1994), 69.

p. 20,   "The two of us . . ." Anthony Sampson, *Mandela: The Authorized Biography* (New York: Vintage Books, 2000), 26.

p. 21,   "This was one of my . . ." Maharaj and Kathrada, *Mandela: The Authorized Portrait*, 22.

p. 22,   "very, very ugly," Chief Jonginyaniso Mtirara, "The Long Walk of Nelson Mandela Interviews: Chief Ndaba Mtirara, Chief Anderson Joyi and Chief Jonginyaniso Mtirara," PBS.org.

p. 22,   "[Nelson] feared to tell . . . " Ibid.

p. 25,   "each and every chief . . ." Chief Ndaba Mtirara, "The Long Walk of Nelson Mandela Interviews: Chief Ndaba Mtirara, Chief Anderson Joyi and Chief Jonginyaniso Mtirara," PBS.org.

Chapter Two: Bound Heart and Soul

p. 29,   "SEND BOYS HOME AT ONCE," Mandela, *Long Walk*, 65.

p. 31,   "Dark City," Sampson, *Mandela*, 35.

p. 31,   "an elder brother . . ." Fatima Meer, *Higher Than Hope: The Authorized Biography of Nelson Mandela* (New York: Harper Perennial, 1990), 29.

p. 31,   "But my landlord . . ." Ibid., 26.

p. 34,   "He never lost his head. . . ." Mandela, *Long Walk*, 95.

p. 34,   "Africa is a black man's . . ." *Reader's Digest Illustrated History of South Africa: The Real Story*, 363.

p. 34,   "My soul yearns. . ." Sampson, *Mandela*, 41.

p. 34   "Within days of our first . . ." Meer, *Higher Than Hope*, 39-40.

p. 35,   "the better class . . ." Sampson, *Mandela*, 36.

p. 35,   "allocated a two-roomed . . ." Meer, *Higher Than Hope*, 40.

p. 36,   "We were heartbroken," Ibid., 41.

p. 37,   "the meticulous organization. . ." Mandela, *Long Walk*, 104.

p. 37,   "I was now bound heart and soul," Ibid., 108.

Chapter Three: Freedom Fighter

p. 43,   "Today it is the Communist Party . . ." Mandela, *Long Walk*, 117.

p. 44,   "democracy, liberty and harmony," *Reader's Digest Illustrated History of South Africa: The Real Story*, 383.

p. 44,   "Bantu differ in many ways . . ." Ibid.

p. 44,   "we stand on the eve . . ." Ibid.

p. 45,   "[T]he spirit of the people . . ." Nelson Mandela, *In His Own Words* (New York: Little, Brown and Company, 2003), 14.

p. 45,   "The camaraderie of our fellow Defiers. . ." Mandela, *Long Walk*, 131.

p. 46,   "I noticed people turning and staring. . ." Mary Benson, *Nelson Mandela: The Man and the Movement* (New York: W.W. Norton & Company, 1994, 1986), 46.

p. 49,   "Chicago of South Africa," *Reader's Digest Illustrated History of South Africa: The Real Story*, 427.

p. 50,   "not only a place . . ." Ibid., 419.

p. 50,   "A freedom fighter learns . . ." Mandela, *Long Walk*, 166.

p. 51,   "suicidal . . . unbearable," Nelson Mandela, *The Struggle Is My Life; His Speeches and Writing Brought Together with Historical Documents and Accounts of Mandela in Prison by Fellow-Prisoners* (New York: Pathfinder Press, 1986), 34-36.

p. 51,   "You can see . . ." Ibid., 42.

p. 52,   "There is no place . . ." Nelson Mandela, *No Easy Walk to Freedom* (Harare, Zimbabwe: Zimbabwe Publishing House, 1965), 47.

p. 52,   "The Nationalist Government . . ." Ibid., 47.

p. 52,   "The school must equip . . ." *Reader's Digest Illustrated History of South Africa: The Real Story*, 379.

p. 53,   "draw up a freedom charter . . ." Ibid., 387.

pp. 53-54, "South Africa belongs. . ." Mandela, *The Struggle Is My Life*, 50.

Chapter Four: On Trial for High Treason

p. 62,   "It was ironic . . ." Mandela, *Long Walk*, 187.

p. 63,   "What distance . . ." *Reader's Digest Illustrated History of South Africa: The Real Story*, 389.

p. 68,   "It is a name. . ." Mandela, *Long Walk*, 226.

p. 68,   "You probably . . ." Meer, *Higher Than Hope*, xv.

p. 68,   "you are called upon . . ." Mandela, *Long Walk*, 234.

p. 69,   "dignity and sincerity," Ibid., 235.

p. 69,   "People fell . . ." Adrian Porter, "62 Africans Die in Race Law Protest," *Washington Post*, March 22, 1960.

p. 69,   "One little boy . . ." Maharaj and Kathrada, *Mandela: The Authorized Portrait*, 88.

p. 69,   "Policemen said later . . ." Porter, "62 Africans Die in Race Law Protest."

pp. 70-71, "The aeroplanes were flying . . ." *Reader's Digest Illustrated History of South Africa: The Real Story*, 403.

p. 72,   "encrusted with dried blood and vomit . . ." Mandela, *Long Walk*, 241.

p. 74,   "After one has been in prison . . ." Ibid., 253.

p. 75,   "We shall say . . ." Ibid., 256.

p. 75,   "In the case of the Treason Trial. . ." Ibid., 260.

Chapter Five: "An Outlaw in My Own Land"

p. 77,   "I became a creature . . ." Mandela, *Long Walk*, 267.

p. 78,   "millions of friends . . . without reservation," Mandela, *The Struggle Is My Life*, 118.

p. 79,   "The attacks . . ." Mandela, *Long Walk*, 271.

p. 80,   "Nonviolence has not failed . . ." Ibid., 273.

p. 80,   "The time comes . . ." Benson, *Nelson Mandela*, 110-111.

p. 81,   "as an outlaw . . . the end of my days," Mandela, *The Struggle Is My Life*, 121.

p. 81,   "firm and unswerving," Gunnar Jahn, "The Nobel Peace Prize 1960—Presentation Speech," http://nobelprize.org/nobel_prizes/peace/laureates/1960/press.html.

p. 82,   "We believe in . . ." Ibid.

p. 82,   "without violence . . . had it so," Ibid.

p. 83,   "bring the government . . ." *Reader's Digest Illustrated History of South Africa: The Real Story*, 410.

p. 84,   "While I gloried . . ." Mandela, *Long Walk*, 303.

p. 84,   "with assurance . . . in your office," Ibid., 305.

p. 84,   "Military training must . . ." Ibid., 306.

Chapter Six: "The Struggle Is My Life"

p. 89,   "Why is it that . . ." Maharaj and Kathrada, *Mandela: The Authorized Portrait*, 113.

p. 90,   "The gloves are off . . ." "South Africa Opens Trial of Mandela," *Washington Post*, October 23, 1962.

p. 91,   "Then our people . . . my conscience," Nelson Mandela, *In His Own Words* (New York: Little, Brown and Company, 2003), 20-24.

p. 94,   "Mandela, you don't . . ." Mandela, *Long Walk*, 350.

p. 95,   "I felt we . . ." Ibid., 362.

p. 95,   "many years of tyranny . . . I am prepared to die" Mandela, *In His Own Words*, 27-42.

p. 97,   "I was prepared . . ." Mandela, *Long Walk*, 373.

p. 98,   "to bow their heads. . ." Ibid., 375.

p. 98,   "People who organize . . ." Ibid.

Chapter Seven: On Robben Island

p. 101,   "Well, you chaps . . ." Mandela, *Long Walk*, 381.

p. 104,   "mental attitude . . . idle thought," Ahmed Kathrada, *Letters from Robben Island: A Selection of Ahmed Kathrada's Prison Correspondence, 1964-1989* (Michigan State University Press, 1999), 45.

p. 105,   "we tend to concentrate . . ." Maharaj and Kathrada, *Mandela: The Authorized Portrait*, 167.

p. 106,   "the years roll by. . ." Kathrada, *Letters from Robben Island*, 71.

p. 106,   "it did not halt . . ." Mandela, *Long Walk*, 444.

p. 107,   "imposing stature . . . communicating," Maharaj and Kathrada, *Mandela: The Authorized Portrait*, 154.

p. 108,   "I never dreamt . . ." Nelson Mandela, *Conversations With Myself* (New York: Farrar, Strauss and Giroux, 2010), 159.

p. 108,   "twenty-four hours . . . new dresses," Ibid., 161.

p. 108,   "I feel as if . . ." Ibid., 183.

p. 108,   "If there was ever . . ." Ibid., 184-185.

p. 108,   "Please advise Nelson Mandela . . ." Ibid., 165.

p. 109,   "left a hole in my heart . . ." Maharaj and Kathrada, *Mandela: The Authorized Portrait*, 156.

p. 109,   "At the time it was . . ." Ibid., 166.

p. 109,   "cordial . . . small talk," Kathrada, *Letters from Robben Island*, 47.

p. 110,   "At some point . . ." *Reader's Digest Illustrated History of South Africa: The Real Story*, 420.

p. 111,   "very diplomatic. . . fit and strong," Benson, *Nelson Mandela*, 185.

p. 113,   "The films were . . ." Mandela, *Long Walk*, 500.

p. 113,   "To hold a newborn . . ." Ibid., 495.

Chapter Eight: "Time to Talk"

p. 115,   "no people . . . that future," Benson, *Nelson Mandela*, 216-217.

p. 116,   "A man can get used to anything. . ." Mandela, *Long Walk*, 510.

p. 116,   "a gentle, caring person," Kathrada, *Letters from Robben Island*, 229.

p. 117,   "it had been . . ." Mandela, *Long Walk*, 517.

p. 118,   "[A]lthough he has . . . weapons of spirit and reason," Egil
            Aarvik, "The Nobel Peace Prize 1984—Presentation Speech,"
            http://nobelprize.org/nobel_prizes/peace/laureates/1984/presen-
            tation-speech.html.

p. 118,   "There is no peace . . . swords into ploughshares," "Desmond
            Tutu—Nobel Lecture," http://nobelprize.org/nobcl_prizes/
            peace/laureates/1984/tutu-lecture.html.

p. 119,   "a moral disgrace," Jesse Jackson, "Speech at the 1984
            Democratic National Convention," http://www.americanrhetoric.
            com/speeches/jessejackson1984dnc.htm.

p. 120,   "when all other . . . not respected," Mandela, *In His Own Words*,
            46-47.

p. 121,   "It was time to talk," Mandela, *Long Walk*, 525.

p. 125,   "as necessary . . ." Ibid., 552.

p. 126,   "Our world . . ." Ibid., 556.

p. 127,   "I came out . . ." Richard Stengel, "Mandela: His 8 Lessons of
            Leadership," *Time*, July 9, 2008.

Chapter Nine: "Never Again"

p. 131,   "Suffering can . . . of his adversary," Maharaj and Kathrada,
            Mandela: The Authorized Portrait, 7.

p. 132,   "Today, my return . . ." Mandela, *Long Walk*, 570.

p. 133,   "The effect of apartheid . . . arrested and jailed," Jon Sawyer,
            "The Cost: Sisulus Finally Free," *St. Louis Post-Dispatch*,
            September 28, 1990.

p. 134,   "We have risen . . ." John Kifner, "The Mandela Visit; Mandela
            Takes His Message to Rally in Yankee Stadium," *New York
            Times*, June 22, 1990.

p. 134,   "During the long years . . ." Tracy Wilkinson and Scott Kraft,
            "Mandela Pleads ANC Cause at Harlem Rally," *Los Angeles
            Times*, June 22, 1990.

pp. 134-135, "To lift sanctions now. . ." Ibid.

p. 135,   "As dramatically . . ." Ibid.

p. 137,   "To deny any person . . ." Nelson Mandela, *Nelson Mandela
            Speaks; Forging a Democratic, Nonracial South Africa* (New
            York: Pathfinder, 1993), 37-41.

p. 137,   "an icon of forgiveness . . . every person," Mandela, *In His Own Words*, 318.

p. 140,   "When your life . . ." Mandela, *Long Walk*, 600.

p. 143,   "This is a watershed . . . with wisdom," Mandela, *Nelson Mandela Speaks*, 236-237.

p. 143,   "like the loneliest man. . ." Mandela, *Long Walk*, 609.

p. 143,   "A mind whose thoughts . . ." Mandela, *In His Own Words*, 489.

p. 144,   "who dared to rise. . . silver or gold," Ibid., 507-510.

p. 146,   "I think we are . . ." Mandela, *Long Walk*, 617.

p. 146,   "I watched, . . free at last!" Mandela, *In His Own Words*, 63.

p. 146,   "not the victory . . ." Ibid., 65.

p. 147,   "[W]e, who were . . . " Ibid., 68-70.

p. 147,   "I can rest . . ." Mandela, *Long Walk*, 625.

Chapter Ten: "Madiba"

p. 157,   "the power . . . " Mandela, *In His Own Words*, 81.

p. 152,   "We can forgive . . ." Sampson, *Mandela*, 521.

pp. 152-153, "The best recompense . . ." Mandela, *In His Own Words*, 81.

p. 153,   "Further construction . . ." Ibid., 135.

p. 154,   "I look forward . . ." Sampson, *Mandela*, 536.

p. 154,   "History will judge. . ." Mandela, *In His Own Words*, 194.

p. 155,   "[T]here is no . . ." Ibid., 167.

p. 155,   "It is in . . . walk continues," Ibid., 172-176.

p. 156,   "AIDS knows . . ." Ibid., 392.

p. 156,   "One issue that . . ." Mandela, *Conversations With Myself*, 410.

p. 156,   "He stood head and shoulders . . ." Ofeibea Quist-Arcton, "Anti-Apartheid Hero Walter Sisulu Dies at 90," AllAfrica.com, May 6, 2003, http://allafrica.com/stories/200305060280.html.

p. 157,   "A man should die . . ." Sampson, *Mandela*, 5.

Bibliography

Benson, Mary. *Nelson Mandela: The Man and the Movement*. New York: W. W. Norton & Company, 1994, 1986.

Kathrada, A. M. (Ahmed). *Letters from Robben Island: A Selection of Ahmed Kathrada's Prison Correspondence, 1964-1989*. Michigan State University Press, 1999.

Machel, Graça. *Impact of Armed Conflict on Children*. UNICEF, 1996. http://www.unicef.org/graca/.

Maharaj, Mac, and Ahmed Kathrada, ed. *Mandela: The Authorized Portrait*. Kansas City, MO: Andrews McMeel Publishing, 2006.

Mandela, Nelson. *In His Own Words*. New York: Little, Brown and Company, 2003.

———. *Conversations With Myself.* New York: Farrar, Straus and Giroux, 2010.

———. *Long Walk to Freedom: The Autobiography of Nelson Mandela*. New York: Little, Brown and Company, 1994, 1995.

———. *Nelson Mandela Speaks; Forging a Democratic, Nonracial South Africa*. New York: Pathfinder, 1993.

———. *No Easy Walk to Freedom*. Harare, Zimbabwe: Zimbabwe Publishing House Ltd., 1965.

———. *The Struggle Is My Life; His Speeches and Writing Brought Together with Historical Documents and Accounts of Mandela in Prison by Fellow-Prisoners*. New York: Pathfinder Press, 1986.

Meer, Fatima. *Higher than Hope: The Authorized Biography of Nelson Mandela*. New York: HarperPerennial, 1990.

Meredith, Martin. *Nelson Mandela: A Biography*. New York: St. Martin's Press, 1997.

Reader's Digest Illustrated History of South Africa: The Real Story. Cape Town: The Reader's Digest Association South Africa Ltd., 1994.

Sampson, Anthony. *Mandela: The Authorized Biography*. New York: Vintage Books, 1999.

Articles and Lectures

Aarvik, Egil. "The Nobel Peace Prize 1984—Presentation Speech." http://nobelprize.org/nobel_prizes/peace/laureates/1984/presentation-speech.html.

Bearak, Barry. "Mandela Misses Day 1 of Games to Mourn." *New York Times*, June 12, 2010.

Bryson, Donna. "South Africans mark Mandela's birthday." *Washington Post*, July 18, 2010.

Collins, Glenn. "For '*Sarafina!*' Cast, Life Without Apartheid." *New York Times*, April 3, 1989.

Delius, Anthony. "Cards Are Stacked Against Africa's Black Pimpernel." *Washington Post*, October 28, 1962.

"8 Convicted of Treason in South African Trial." *Washington Post*, June 12, 1964.

Gall, Henderson. "Banned Africa Leader Mandela Put on Trial." *Washington Post*, October 1962.

Jackson, Jesse. "Speech at the 1984 Democratic National Convention." http://www.americanrhetoric.com/speeches/jessejackson1984dnc.htm.

Jahn, Gunnar. "The Nobel Peace Prize 1960—Presentation Speech." http://nobelprize.org/nobel_prizes/peace/laureates/1960/press.html.

Kavanagh, Christopher. "S. African Sabotage Tactics Cited." *Washington Post*, April 27, 1964.

Kennedy, Helen. "Nelson Mandela attends World Cup Final: Anti-apartheid Leader Draws Tears, Joy From Packed Crowd." *New York Daily News*, July 11, 2010.

Kifner, John. "The Mandela Visit; Mandela Takes His Message To Rally in Yankee Stadium." *New York Times*, June 22, 1990.

"Letters from the Darkness." *Sunday Times of London*, October 10, 2010.

Luthuli, Albert. "Nobel Lecture." http://nobelprize.org/nobel_prizes/peace/laureates/1960/lutuli-lecture.html.

Mandela, Nelson. "Acceptance and Nobel Lecture 1993." http://nobelprize.org/nobel_prizes/peace/laureates/1993/mandela-lecture.html.

Mandela, Nelson. "The Sacred Warrior." *Time*, December 31, 1999.

McSmith, Andy. "Oliver Tambo: The Exile." *Independent*, October 15, 2007.

"Nelson Mandela Thanks UN for Efforts to Secure His Release."
UN Chronicle, September 1990.

"'Pimpernel' Mandela Is Jailed 5 Years in South Africa Trial." *Washington Post*, November 8, 1962.

Porter, Adrian. "62 Africans Die in Race Law Protest." *Washington Post*, March 22, 1960.

Quist-Arcton, Ofeibea. "Anti-Apartheid Hero Walter Sisulu dies at 90." AllAfrica.com, May 6, 2003. http://allafrica.com/stories/200305060280.html.

Robinson, Stephen. "Man Behind the Martyr." *Sunday Times of London*, June 13, 2010.

Sawyer, Jon. "The Cost: Sisulus Finally Free." *St. Louis Post-Dispatch*, September 28, 1990.

———. "Leaders Blamed for S. African Violence." *St. Louis Post-Dispatch*, September 23, 1990.

———. "New York Cheers Mandela." *St. Louis Post-Dispatch*, June 21, 1990.

———. "Pessimism Haunts S. Africa." *St. Louis Post-Dispatch*, September 16, 1990.

———. "Racialists Expect Civil War." *St. Louis Post-Dispatch*, September 30, 1990.

"South Africa Opens Trial of Mandela." *Washington Post*, October 23, 1962.

Snyman, Mia. "SAfricans split on Mandela's attendance at opening." *Seattle Times*, June 7, 2010.

Tutu, Desmond. "Nobel Lecture." http://nobelprize.org/nobel_prizes/peace/laureates/1984/tutu-lecture.html.

Wilkinson, Tracy, and Scott Kraft. "Mandela Pleads ANC Cause at Harlem Rally." *Los Angeles Times*, June 22, 1990.

Web sites

http://www.nelsonmandelachildrensfund.com
Nelson Mandela Children's Fund

The Children's Fund oversees a Youth Parliament and youth clubs, works with children affected by HIV/AIDS, and encourages dialogue to establish more leadership roles for women. They have also started a major fundraising campaign for a children's hospital.

http://www.nelsonmandela.org
Nelson Mandela Foundation

The Center of Memory and Dialogue, established by the foundation, celebrates the life of Mandela—maintaining an extensive archive and promoting dialogue on issues related to justice, human rights, health, and social issues, such as HIV prevention.

The foundation also sponsors an annual lecture. Guest lecturers have included Chilean author Ariel Dorfman, Liberian president Ellen Johnson-Sirleaf, United Nations Secretary-General Kofi Annan, President Bill Clinton, Archbishop Desmond Tutu, and environmentalist Wangari Mathai.

http://www.anc.org.za
African National Congress

The official Web site of the African National Congress, the majority party in the South African government, includes a repository of articles, speeches, and manifestos related to the history of the ANC.

http://www.pbs.org/wgbh/pages/frontline/shows/mandela
"The Long Walk of Nelson Mandela: An Intimate Portrait of One of the 20th Century's Greatest Leaders."

PBS has put together on this site extensive coverage of Mandela's life and times. There are stories and insights from Mandela's closest colleagues, fellow prisoners, friends, and political adversaries; interviews with two of his chief biographers, Richard Stengel and Anthony Sampson; and interviews with three chiefs from Mandela's clan in the Eastern Cape region.

http://cyberschoolbus.un.org/discrim/race
United Nations Cyberschoolbus

The United Nations has a full curriculum for interested learners on Discrimination Based on Race, and it includes lessons on apartheid and an apartheid timeline.

Index

possible death sentence, 94, 97-98

presidency, 146, 149, 151, 154-156

in prison, 89, 91-92, 98, 101-113, 115-117, 121, 124

release from prison, 126-127

in the U.S., 134-137

and violence, 67, 78-79, 81, 119-121

Mandela, Nosekeni, Fanny (mother), 10-12, 14, 61, *98*, 107

Mandela, Thembikile (son), 36, 63-64, 108-109

Mandela, Winnie (second wife), 65-68, *66,* 74-75, 87-89, *90,* 94, 98, *98,* 103, 106, 108, 111-113, 116-117, 127, *128-129,* 131-132, *133,* 139-140

Mandela, Zenani (daughter), 68, 113

Mandela, Zindziswa (daughter), 75, 111-112, 119, *120*

martial law, 46, 72, 121-122, 134

Matanzima, Kaiser, 20, 68

Matthews, Z. K., 53

Mbeki, Govan, 95, 97

Mbeki, Thabo, 123, 146, 151, 153-154, *155*

Mhlaba, Raymond, 97, 116, 121-122, 125

MK (military organization), 80-82, 84, 92-96, 142

Mlangeni, Andrew, 97, 116, 122, 125

Moroka, James, 41, 44, *47*

Motsoaledi, Elias, 97

Mphakanyiswa, Gadla (father), 10-12

Murray, Andrew, 64-65

naming traditions, 24-25

Natal Indian Congress, 36-37, *37*

National Action Council, 53

National Day of Protest, 43-44

National Party, 38-39, 40, 43-44, 46, 49-51, 125, 132, 139, 142, 144

Natives Act, 28

Nehru, Jawaharlal, 51, 115-116

Ninety Day Dentention Law, 92

Nobel Peace Prize, 81-82, 118, 144

nonviolent resistance, 37, 41, 44-45, 47, 50, 75, 80, 137-138

Operation Mayibuye, 95

Pan-African Conference, 82, 84

Pan Africanist Congress, 69

Pass Laws Act, 28

pass system, 39, 67, 69, 72

Paton, Alan, 63, 98-99, *99*

political prisoners, 92, 97, 103, 106-107, 116, 125-126, 137

Pollsmoor prison, 116-117, 121, 124

Pretoria Minute, 137

Progressive Party, 106

Public Safety Act, 46

racial segregation, 28, 33, 39-40, 43-44, 46, 51-52, 99, 122, 125

Radebe, Gaur, 29, 32-33

Ramaphosa, Cyril, 152

Photo Credits

All images used in this book that are not in the public domain are credited in the listing that follows:

cover: Getty Images

4-5: Courtesy of perry-Castenada Library Map Collection

13: Top Photo: Duggan-Cronin Collection, McGregor Museum, Kimberley. Bottom: Moravian Archives Herrnhut, Germany, BOX-SAO-1-01526

14: Benedicte Kurzen/VII Network, Corbis

17: Moravan Archives, Herrnhut, Germany, BOX-SAO-00744a

21: Cory Library/Cory Library/Africa Media Online

23: Moravian Archives, Herrnhut, Germany: Top left photo (BOX-SAO-7-10002), top right (BOX-SAO-2-06983), bottom (BOX-SAO-2-06982).

30: Associated Press

32: Courtesy of Library of Congress

35: Maxppp/Landov

38: University of Stellenbosch

47: Getty Images

49: Baileys Archive/africanpictures/The Image Works

54-55: Baileys Archive/africanpictures/ The Image Works

64: Associated Press

66: Reuters/Landov

70-71: Pictorial Press Ltd./Alamy

73: Associated Press

74: Reuters/Landov

79: Associated Press

83: Baileys Archive/africanpictures/ The Image Works

85: Courtesy of Eric Gaba

88: Associated Press

90: Associated Press

96: Associated Press

98: TopFoto/The Image Works

102: Associated Press

105: David Parker/Alamy

107: Gallo Images/Alamy

110: Gamma-Keystone via Getty Images

117: Associated Press

118: Associated Press

120: Associated Press

123: Associated Press

126: Associated Press

128-129: Associated Press

132: Associated Press

135: Associated Press

136: Associated Press

139: Associated Press

141: Associated Press

142: Associated Press

145: Associated Press

147: Associated Press

150: Associated Press

155: Associated Press

157: Reuters/Radu Sigheti/Landov

158: Everett Collection Inc./Alamy